Best wishes to a lovely Lady

[illegible]

Cowboys, Cooks, and Catastrophes

Cowboys, Cooks, and Catastrophes

By Reba Pierce Cunningham

Illustrated by Bud McCaulley

The CAXTON PRINTERS, Ltd.
Caldwell, Idaho
1988

Illustrated By Bud McCaulley

Library of Congress Cataloging-in-Publication Data

Cunningham, Reba Pierce.
Cowboys, cooks, and catastrophes.

1. Cunningham, Reba Pierce.
2. Ranchers wives—Wyoming—Biography. 3. Ranch life
—Wyoming—Biography. I. Title.
F596.C97 1985 978.7'033'0924 [B] 85-18615
ISBN 0-935269-01-0

The following chapters appeared in similar form in *True West* and *Frontier Times* magazines: "Pat"; "Mollie"; "Gertie"; "Maggie"; "Pete, Old Buck, and I"; "Lonelyhearts, Waterwagons, and Robbery at the N Bar N"; "Luella"; "Nellie White, Little Mother of the N Bar N"; and "Christmas at the N Bar N."

Lithographed and bound in the United States of America by
The CAXTON PRINTERS, Ltd., Caldwell, Idaho USA
150262

For the Hungry Children of the World

Contents

Chapter

Cowboys, Cooks, and Catastrophes

1

Pat

In 1932 my husband, John, and I and our three-year-old son, Tommy, left the cornfields of Iowa to manage a cattle spread near Buffalo, Wyoming. When my father got wind of our decision he took me aside and warned me of the dangers I would have to face in that God-forsaken country. "You'll be living with cowboys as wild as the broncos they ride, and I wouldn't be surprised if some of them eat grass."

He went on to tell me about Cattle Kate, who had been hanged in Wyoming for stealing cattle. After they hanged her, they found only a few milk cows on her small range. If that were not enough to make chills run up and down my spine, he went on to tell me other gruesome stories that happened long ago in that wild and untamed land. Father was careful not to omit any of the details.

It was little wonder that I was filled with apprehension when we arrived at the ranch.

My husband and little Tommy had gone to explore the corrals and barns, and I was left standing on the porch of the old log house that was to be my home. I stood for a moment in the evening twilight and listened to the yapping of a coyote on a distant hill. The cold wind blowing in from the Big Horn Mountains brought a twinge of homesickness to my heart.

As I opened the door I was met by a bow-legged old cowboy. He was smoking a corncob pipe. In the pocket of his vest was a sack of Bull Durham. Around his neck he wore a flowing red scarf. I knew he had put on his best bib and tucker just to meet me.

The old man had a broad smile and twinkling blue eyes. What I could see of his face through its heavy growth of gray whiskers was friendly. Apparently he was a self-appointed envoy welcoming me to my new home on the range. For a moment the old cowboy stared at me. Then his face split into a grin and a tooth peeked out from between the gray whiskers.

"I'm Pat," he announced. "I'll betcha yore the boss's wife. My, you ain't no bigger'n a bar a soap. Come now, I'll show you 'round the cabin."

He held out a hand with two missing fingers. It was gnarled and calloused but almost feminine, and when I took it I could sense its tenderness. Pat shook my hand so long that when he gave it back to me my arm was a limp, lifeless thing.

The cabin consisted of five small rooms. Pat took his time to point out the "settin" room, as he called it. Blood and blond hair covered the floor. When he noticed my look of horror, he quickly explained, "Ain't no female been murdered here, ma'am. The boys just been skinnin' a coyote to pass away the time."

The walls of one of the bedrooms were smeared with large brown patches, from which tiny streams flowed down to the floor. Pat's explanation was simple. Last night the cowhands had engaged in a hilarious tobacco spitting contest.

In the opposite corner I noticed a large sack of grain, its contents strewn across the floor. The old cowboy followed my gaze. "Oh, that. Ma'am, packrats been a-feedin' there. If you see one of 'em runnin' around, don't get scared." I drew my skirt close about me. "They won't bite; they'll just want to be your friend.

"They're really fair little critters. They won't take nothin' from you 'less they bring somethin' back. If they take a spoon or a piece of cloth or one of your combs, they'll bring you back somethin' like a pine cone or a bone or a feather." Pat took another puff on his pipe and motioned for me to follow.

In another room we ran on to a hound dog leisurely nursing six hungry puppies. "She won't hurt you ma'am. That's Lulu Belle. The old fool sneaked in here last night and had a mess a pups. Hungry little devils, ain't they? She belongs to one of the boys. When he knew you was a-comin', he decided to give Lulu Bell and her little puppies to you." How generous of the cowboy! But the last thing I needed at the moment was a skinny hound dog and her six ravenous pups.

There was no sign of a bathroom. "That's just fine," I thought. "Next winter I'll have to trudge through the snow to one of the little buildings out back. And I'll have to carry my own wash water."

In the back of the cabin was a dug-out basement. As long as my constitution had carried me this far, I might as well go the rest of the way and see what lurked in the basement's musty confines. I followed Pat down the dirt steps, and my nose directed me to a huge carcass of dressed beef. It was hung from the ceiling with a lariat rope. I didn't know how old the carcass was, but it had grown whiskers.

All the while Pat remained mute. Perhaps he knew more about the carcass than he cared to divulge. I couldn't help but wonder if the dressed beef had not been sneaked into the cave in anticipation of a steak fry at some secret rendezvous.

As we walked back up the steps, something crawled across my foot.

I screamed. "Is it a rattlesnake, Pat?"

"No, ma'am, it ain't. Jus' a innocent little lizard. Won't hurt you none, ma'am."

Pat insisted I take a look into the kitchen. It was furnished with a crude table, two chairs, and a cupboard that ran along one wall. Although I was curious about the cupboard's contents, I did not have the courage to open its doors.

Before we left the kitchen, I noticed a bright object on the floor. Thinking it would make a pretty knocker for the front door, I picked it up and held it out for Pat to see. But I promptly dropped it when he told me he thought one of the boys picked it up near the cemetery.

"You know, ma'am," he said, "don't think you'd want to use that. Looks to me like a coffin handle."

The old cowboy noticed my tears. He looked at me for a moment. Then from somewhere in the recesses of his faded wool pants he brought forth a red bandana. "Now, ma'am, you jus' dry them purty blue eyes a yourn, and we'll go up and meet the cook and the boys at the cookhouse. They been anxious to meet you and it's 'bout supper time."

In a clump of sage along the path back of the cookhouse, I noticed discarded whiskey bottles as thick as apple butter.

The cookhouse was a long shed-like building. Pat explained it was made up of three rooms—a large kitchen, an adjoining bedroom for the cook, and a dining room with long wooden tables and benches large enough to accommodate thirty hungry cowhands.

I met John and Tommy at the kitchen door and walked with them into the cookhouse. The cook was busy dishing up enormous bowls of potatoes and gravy and filling large platters with roast beef. She was a big-boned woman with straggly gray hair pulled back into a knot at the back of her head. Her face was deeply lined. She looked tired.

She placed the food on the tables of the dining room before acknowledging our presence. With a brief "howdy," she announced, "I'm leavin' tonight and want my wages."

John tried to explain that we had just arrived. He would appreciate it if she would reconsider and stay on at least until he had time to hire another cook. But she was determined to leave, so he promised her, "You come to my office in the morning and I'll give you your time."

Pat gave us a brief introduction to the thirty cowhands sitting around the tables. "Boys, I want you to meet our new boss, his missis and their little kid."

The cowboys Pat said were so eager to meet me barely stopped their eating long enough to say "howdy," and that was the extent of their greeting.

As John, Tommy, and I walked down to the log house we were all deep in thought. Even Tommy was silent for once.

The moon was just coming up and its light softened the unsightly buildings all about us. Peace rested over the valley of the Big Horn Mountains like a gentle benediction. I stopped a moment to take in all that beauty. But I was brought out of my reverie when John asked, "Do you know the cook quit?"

I nodded.

"You realize, of course, these cowhands work hard and have to be well fed."

I nodded again and agreed.

"Do you know who is going to get up at 4:30 in the morning to cook their breakfast?"

"I haven't the foggiest idea."

He walked over, pointed a finger under my nose, and announced in no uncertain terms, "You, that's who."

"Me? You can't be serious."

"I was never more serious in my life. You'll have to do the cooking until I have time to look over the outfit and hire a cook. You have no alternative."

With welling emotions, I followed him and Tommy down to the log house. I was angry and frightened. A good speech was beginning to jell. "If you think you are going to make a charwoman out of me, you are out of your mind. I didn't come all the way to Wyoming to cook for thirty bow-legged cowhands who play nursemaid to five thousand bawling cows on a spread that runs from here to eternity. . . ." It would have been a very fine speech, but at the moment I was too tired to deliver it.

Our furniture had not arrived, so John brought blankets and pillows from our car and we bedded down for the night on the floor of the "settin'" room. Someone had cleaned out the grain, and, I hoped, the packrats. Lulu Belle and her brood were also missing. I lay on the hard floor trying to decide what to do. Should I sneak out with Tommy, get in the car and head back to Iowa? Or should I get up at 4:30 in the morning and try to tackle a job I knew was impossible for me? In Iowa I had been buying steak by the pound and pork by the chop, but cooking for thirty cowhands was. . .I drifted off to sleep.

I was awakened suddenly by John's flashing a light in my face and pointing to his watch. "It's four-thirty. You'd better get started. I see a light in the cookhouse and the boys will soon be coming in for breakfast. I'll join you later."

I wanted to wring his neck. Instead I dragged my weary bones from the floor and staggered up to the cookhouse. When I opened the door I was greeted by a fire that had already been started in the range. It was red hot and just waiting for me. I sat down on a kitchen chair, my thoughts briny as a salt lick. Soon all the pent-up anger left me and I couldn't hold back my tears.

Suddenly I heard footsteps. The door was thrown open, and through my tears I saw Pat.

"Ma'am, I jus' figgered you might need some help. I used to be a roundup cook. When we need help at the cookhouse, I still wrangle the pots and pans."

I arose from my chair and cried out, "Help!"

Out came the red bandana again, and Pat handed it over to me. "Now, you jus' stop yore cryin' and set the tables and I'll git busy on them flapjacks. On the roundup we called them saddle blankets."

Pat went to the cupboard and pulled out a dishpan big enough for me to take a bath in. He filled it with flour and something called "sourdough" that he dipped out of a keg back of the stove. "You know, ma'am, I have to keep a rattlesnake in that keg at all times jus' to keep that dough a workin'."

After Pat had stirred the contents of the pan to his satisfaction, he put three huge skillets and three long griddles on the stove. While they were heating he brought two mammoth coffee pots out from behind the stove and made the coffee. "Want to know how I make my coffee?"

I nodded.

"I make mine outa one cup a coffee to four cups a spring water. When it'll float my six-shooter, I know it's 'bout right. Sometimes on the roundup, when I emptied the grounds I could find most anythin'—my dishrag, corncob pipe or maybe a little field mouse had crawled in. But, shucks, the boys never knew the difference."

Pat pushed the coffee pots to the back of the stove and took time out to tell me something more about his coffee making on the roundup. "Yep, them early days on the roundup, no cowpuncher could a-rode a bronc, nor a chuckwagon a-bumped over the ranges without it. 'Kewpons' come with every sack of Arbuckles coffee and a stick of peppermint candy. The sacks were purty, too, with a flyin' angel wearin' a red scarf on 'em. And you know what, ma'am? One time I had enough of the 'kewpons' to git me a talkin' machine with a big pink horn that looked jus' like a mornin' glory. The boys jus' couldn't believe all that music could come out a that horn and from the little round disk that went round and round. Ever night they would sit 'round on their haunches and listen to 'The Arkansas Traveler.' But their favorite was, 'The Bird on Nellie's Hat.'

"Well," he stopped for a moment, and I knew he was thinking of his old roundup days. "Guess I better get a-goin' with the breakfast." He went to the huge icebox outside and came back dragging what looked like half a cow. He began slicing off large steaks, rolling them in flour and placing them in hot fat in the skillets.

Their aroma was tantalizing, and I suddenly realized I was hungry. The cowhands, too, must have smelled the coffee and frying steak, for they soon began to amble into the dining room. As each one passed, he glanced shyly at me and said, "Howdy, ma'am."

John came in later with sleepy-eyed Tommy at his heels. "How you doing?" he asked me. He didn't seem the least perturbed to see Pat in the kitchen.

"Oh, I'm getting along just fine and dandy." I'd show him!

Later I found an opportune time to settle this job as ranch cook once and for all. The dishes were out of the way; Pat had gone back to the bunkhouse; and the cowhands were off to the corrals to saddle up for the day. "John, I'll make a bargain with you. Although I have plenty to do just trying to convert this old log house into a decent home, I'll take over this job at the cookhouse if you have Pat do the cooking."

He looked surprised. I was sure he was waiting for me to scream, have hysterics, or walk out. "Why, sure thing. . . that's great. I'll get a hand to take Pat's place, and I promise you I'll hire a cook as soon as I can find one."

He thought for a moment and added, "Honey, I think I'll turn the job over to you." I wasn't too enthusiastic about that idea. But what was a wife for? Faintly I recalled my marriage vows—for better or for worse.

That night after the dishes were done and Pat had gone back to the bunkhouse, I decided to surprise him by starting the next day's dinner. I recalled my home economics teacher had taught us that beans gave energy. Who needed more vim and vigor than our thirty cowhands? I rushed for the same huge pan Pat had used for his flapjacks. I hurried to the supply room and filled the pan full of beans from a hundred pound sack.

I couldn't remember ever cooking beans. My knowledge of them was limited to the variety that came in a can labeled *Van Camps*. But I did know dried beans had to be soaked overnight before they could be cooked. Proud of myself, I finished preparing the beans and tripped down to the old log house.

John and Tommy were both asleep when I arrived. I slipped between the blankets on the hard floor and snuggled down to sleep, thinking I would show that husband of mine. "You dish it out, and I can take it!"

Getting up the next morning was not quite as big a chore as it had been the day before. The light was again on at the cookhouse, and a fire had been laid. But I was not prepared for the sight that met me. The beans had swollen all out of proportion, and they were everywhere. They had escaped from the pan, run across the kitchen table, crawled along the floor, and arrived at the door just in time to bid me "Good morning!"

As I hunted frantically for pans to hold all those beans, Pat walked through the door. From his expression I could see he had seen such beans before. He looked at me, looked at the beans, looked back at me, and shook his shaggy gray head. "Ma'am," he said, "them's a hell of a lot of beans."

Pat taught me how to cook those beans so they wouldn't

rattle on our plates. We had bean soup, beans and ham hocks, and beans with salt pork and molasses. And Pat's baked beans were unimaginably delicious. Those beans were consumed in two days. Cowhands who had complained about eating beans, calling them "whistle berries," downed Pat's with gusto and asked for more.

In the three weeks Pat cooked for us he refused to relinquish his corncob pipe or floursack apron. But that didn't bother me. In his own way, he was trying to live again his old days on the roundup.

Pat taught me many things about the culinary art those three weeks at the cookhouse. He was the teacher, I the pupil—always. The first time I ate one of his baking powder biscuits, I remained tight-lipped about having majored in home economics. It was light as a powder puff. I didn't know whether to eat it or sneak away with it to powder my nose.

The cowhands even prevailed on Pat to make his famous "son-of-a-bitch stew." (When ladies were present, it was referred to as "son-of-a-gun.") Pat promised he would make it if they would come up with a four-to-six-month-old calf that hadn't been weaned. With thousands of them bawling alongside their mothers on the range, that was no problem.

Pat got out his old Dutch oven and made the stew for which the West was famous. The calf was killed and dressed and brought to the cookhouse. The tongue was skinned. It, the liver, heart, sweetbreads, marrow gut, and brains were the ingredients. The marrow gut is not really a gut but a strip of marrow found in the suckling calf.

Pat cut everything except the brains into small pieces. The cubed ingredients were rolled in flour and browned in fat in the Dutch oven. A little water was added and it was all cooked until very tender. The brains were added for thickening. The result: a mouth-watering stew. That was the only time we ever had the son-of-a-bitch-of-a-stew, as no other cook could prepare it. We all knew Pat had extended himself to make the stew as a favor to us.

We later learned there had never been a better roundup cook than Pat. He was famous for turning out "fancy" grub. As the cowboys expressed it, a king's table could not have held any more tantalizing grub than Pat put on ours.

I had to have the "receipt" for Pat's biscuits and finally one day came right out and asked for it. He was pleased to give it. A dishpan full of flour, so many handfuls of lard, a smidgeon of this and a smidgeon of that and several pinches of so-and-so. Somehow, I've never had the courage to bake them.

Pat was anxious to get to putting in his garden and setting his hens. So it was up to me to get busy and find a cook.

I came up with Mollie.

2

Mollie

Mollie had been cooking for a dude ranch in our vicinity. I heard she wanted to leave, so I went to see her and hired her to cook for our thirty cowhands at the N Bar N.

Mollie was fat, with buxom curves both fore and aft. She waddled. But beneath that mountain of fat beat a heart kind and generous. She wore her coal-black hair in a huge knot at the nape of her neck. Her nose, slightly hooked, reminded me of the miller in Chaucer's *Canterbury Tales*. For on her nose there grew a wart and on this wart there grew a hair.

With a shoebox in one hand and a banged-up suitcase in the other, Mollie arrived to take over management of the cookhouse. As time went on, we realized we would never see her in any hat other than the one she wore that first night. Its material was black crepe, over which had been sewed rows of horsehair braid. On the front bobbed three red roses. We could only speculate on the hat's original shape, as it had been twisted and turned so many times to conform with changing styles.

After the first frost, she replaced the red roses with three green feathers. At the first sign of spring, off came the feathers and on went the roses.

A few mornings after Mollie arrived she banged on my kitchen door. "Could you come up, ma'am, and help me with my corset?" she asked. "I'm expecting company and I want to look pretty."

The corset was a faded pink contraption with countless stays and dangling garters. Undaunted I tried to hook it around her massive form. It was sizes too small, but she set her jaws, gritted her teeth, pulled in her stomach, and yelled for me to go to work.

The way I had to stuff her rolling bulk into that corset was incredible. I pulled and tugged until her bosom hugged her tonsils. Surely she would have popped with the least provocation.

Mollie refused to attend any function, great or small, casual or momentous, without both of us going through the agony of putting on her corset. "Ma'am," she insisted, "I hope I never lose my pride."

The slightest incident could send Mollie into a rage of profanity. Swearing came as naturally to Mollie as breathing. But at the same time she was cursing, she might also be sewing buttons on a cowboy's shirt or baking a cake for his birthday. Because she was also such a marvelous cook, we did everything possible to keep her contented and turned our heads to ignore her tantrums.

Mollie had been cooking for us only two weeks when I made a startling discovery. As I was walking to the cookhouse to get her grocery list one morning, I heard voices coming from her bedroom window. One, high-pitched and feminine would ask a question. The other, low and masculine, would answer it. I knew Mollie must be having an affair with a man in her bedroom.

I walked into the kitchen and called, "Mollie, I'm here to get your grocery list." When she came out of the bedroom I could see she had been alone. Then I realized Mollie talked to herself when she was alone. Perhaps it was her only source of entertainment.

The first thing I noticed about Mollie's cooking was how careful she was to balance our diet with vegetables from Pat's garden. She always came up with salads and pickles exciting and delicious. There were dishes the cowboys had never heard of but downed with relish.

One morning as she shelled fresh peas, I complimented her on that. "These vegetables are full of vitamins, Mollie, something we all need."

She stopped shelling peas and looked at me as though I had gone mildly insane. "Vivamins?" she asked. "Never heard of them. But I suppose they must be good for us if you say so."

Mollie never wasted anything. She used each morsel with ingenuity. Goodness and quality, however, were never sacrificed. Mollie could transform ordinary edibles into culinary delights. In addition to cream and butter, fresh vegetables and good meat, which we could easily supply, Mollie demanded rarities such as cake flour, nuts, and chocolate. But we never hesitated to buy them once we tasted the results in her cakes, pies, and other good foods. Her Big Horn Mountain Cake was a favorite with the cowhands. They named it because its many black walnuts reminded them of the rocks on the Big Horn Mountains. She made it on special occasions like birthdays and holidays or when one of them was ill or injured. It contained the unusual combination of black walnuts and caraway seeds. The hands liked to tease her by observing that the seeds must be mouse droppings.

When Mollie baked a cowboy his cake it was his privilege to share it with anyone he chose. I often wondered if a cowhand didn't occasionally fake a cold or a sore toe or complain of most anything, just to get Mollie to bake him a cake. If she ever thought that was the case, she never let on.

Regardless of her quick temper, the cowhands all loved and respected Mollie. Pat seemed especially fond of her. I sometimes thought the two of them might be carrying on a secret romance. I decided only time would tell, but I never did find out.

Sometimes I've suspected all the ranch cooks in the West had something "ailin.'" Mollie had been working for us only a short time when I learned she had an "ailin' yutress." In addition to all her other troubles she had to cope with that. I felt sorry for her, so I went to town and asked the druggist if he could recommend anything. He thought he might have a bottle of Lydia Pinkham's Female Tonic stored away somewhere. He found it in his storeroom, dusted it off, and I purchased it for Mollie. She was grateful and took a few long swigs from the bottle.

At the time, I had no idea how important Mollie's ailin' yutress would become to the welfare of our outfit. She could predict when a thunderstorm was brewing by the way it acted up. We all ignored the weather reports and relied entirely on the state of Mollie's health. First thing each morning the boys would ask her how she felt. If the answer was "puny" we were in for a terrible storm. Riding the range that day, they would have their slickers tied down behind their saddles and be prepared for a downpour. In the winter, they would be positive a blizzard was on the way and would never leave without their sheepskin coats.

I had a sneaking suspicion that Mollie used her ailment to her best advantage, getting sympathy and favors from us all. But so long as she kept the outfit well-fed, we never complained.

One Monday morning Mollie "yoo-hooed" to me through the screen door to my kitchen. She asked to take my large Mexican basket to Pat's garden and gather the day's vegetables. Pat was busy helping Pete fix fence and didn't have time to pick them.

The basket was large-lipped and commodious. Mollie had so few nice things of her own that I was glad to lend it to her. She swung it over her arm and went merrily on her way.

"Mollie certainly is happy this morning," I said to myself as I flipped the top crust on a cherry pie and popped it into the oven.

Later Pat told me in detail what transpired next. Her basket already half-full of vegetables, Mollie was reaching down to cut a head of cabbage when she saw it. A large skunk was walking leisurely by, hunting bugs for his dinner.

Mollie screamed for help and then screamed again when the startled skunk high-tailed it straight in her direction. She dropped the Mexican basket and lumbered to the barbed wire fence. But when she tried to scramble over it, her ruffled white underpants caught in the wires.

The more she tried to liberate herself, the more entangled she became. Pat and Pete, who were fixing fence nearby, saw her predicament. But they couldn't stop laughing and took their time going to her rescue. First she cursed Pete, and then she hurled a string of profanity at Pat. Everytime she heard the rustle of a cabbage she screamed again and redoubled her efforts to extract herself from the fence.

Hearing Mollie's screams, I rushed to her aid. I fell to my hands and knees to free her from the barbed wire. But before Pat and Pete could help us the skunk made a beeline in our direction. He raised his white-streaked tail, gave the danger signal, and let it go.

Mollie screamed a final blood-curdling scream. Then with a terrific lunge she freed herself from the fence. She leap-frogged over my back and landed on the ground with a thud.

Mollie was up in a twinkling, huffing, puffing, and cursing her way to the cookhouse. But a white flag of truce from her ruffled drawers clung to the fence, waving in the morning breeze.

I laughed and laughed at Mollie fleeing from the skunk. What a funny sight she was! But then I realized I was running, too.

That night at the supper table, I told John of Mollie's skirmish with the skunk. I had never seen anything so funny in my life. When I recalled the white patch of Mollie's pants waving on the fence, I sighed and started laughing all over again.

John looked up at me from his second piece of cherry pie and grinned. "You won't think it's so hilarious when you get a whiff of your Mexican basket."

Where the roundup cooks wielded a six-shooter to keep the cowhands in line, Mollie wielded her cast iron skillet. If she even sensed a potential complaint, all she had to do was to get out the skillet, walk into the dining room, slam it down on the table, unleash a torrent of cuss words, and the trouble ended.

Mollie always ate Sunday dinner with the outfit. One particular Sunday was Pat's birthday, and she had prepared his favorite dinner of chicken and noodles. Mollie's noodles had to be rolled paper thin and cut into tiny pieces. She was just as choosy about the hens she used for the broth. They must be young and fat. And she insisted on using hens that had been scratching in the corral because, she claimed, they had the best flavor.

Mollie was in a foul mood that Sunday when she

prepared the hens. The first one Pat brought to the cookhouse was not quite dead. When she poured the boiling water over it, the hen let out a squawk, jumped out of the pail, and flew into Mollie's bedroom. It landed on the head of her bed.

Mollie unlimbered some of her deadliest vocabulary and screamed for Pat to help her catch that so-and-so of a hen.

Pat had to carry out the execution again.

So it was that when Mollie took her Sunday place at the head of the table she was not in the best of moods. While she ate, a piece of noodle attached itself to the wart on the end of her nose. It refused to leave. Unaware of it, Mollie went on eating.

The cowhands began to snicker and nudge one another. After dinner, Mollie called Pat aside and demanded to know what had caused all the commotion. Gentleman that he was, Pat plucked the noodle from the wart. Mollie cussed one cowhand and then another, every one in turn. Never, she threatened, would she ever sew another button on a cowhand's shirt or bake another birthday cake. To think they could have let her eat her Sunday dinner with a noodle clinging to her nose!

But Mollie could never stay angry long. The next day she was baking pies for the outfit. And that evening she unintentionally evened the score.

Some of the hands riding in the mountains had found a thick patch of red raspberries. They got off their horses and picked berries until their hats were filled to the brim. The berries were given to Mollie to be baked in pies.

The big-hearted cook was delighted with the offering, baked the pies that day, and set them on the window ledge to cool. When she brought the pies back in, however, she let loose another batch of profanity. A wandering colony of ants had discovered the tempting pastries. Having found them to their liking, they were now enjoying their feast.

Mollie brought the pies inside and wiped away the ants.

But she could do nothing about the ones drowned in the sweet red juice.

What the boys didn't know wouldn't hurt them. Mollie cut the pies and put them on the supper table.

Mollie cooked at the N Bar N for six months, and we came to regard her as a permanent fixture. So long as she was queen of the cookhouse, we never worried about keeping the outfit fed.

During all those months, Mollie never received a bit of mail. So when the mailman left a letter for her in the ranch box, I was deeply concerned. I took it to the cookhouse and gave it to her. She eyed it a moment. Then, for the first time, I saw tears in her eyes.

Mollie was scarcely able to cook supper for the boys that night. Later on in the evening she lumbered down to see me. When I answered her knock, she burst out, "I've got to leave, ma'am. I'll be going in the morning." She put her big arms around me and cried. "You and the boss and the boys been awful good to me." Finally she turned away, dragged her enormous body out of the kitchen, and huffed and puffed back to the cookhouse.

When the cowboys heard Mollie was leaving, they were dumbfounded. What was the message that had so upset her? Would we ever know?

We had never learned a thing about Mollie's private life. Now we didn't dare ask. We all agreed she was a woman of mystery. Her attire and mannerisms certainly did not match her elegant cuisine. At some time or another she must have cooked for people of wealth, or perhaps for royalty.

Had an estranged husband begged her to return? Had another outfit offered her more money? Had she lost a fine position and been relegated to the role of ranch cook? Did she have a family?

Questions, questions, questions—all unanswered! By the cowboy's grapevine we did hear one rumor that Mollie had a daughter living in a sporting house in Denver. But that just raised more questions. What kind of trouble was Mollie's daughter in? Had she appealed to her mother for help?

We all wished the letter had never come.

The last time we saw Mollie, she wedged her huge body in beside the driver of our ranch truck and waved goodbye, the three red roses on her hat swaying in unison.

She was gone, but we would never forget her. Long would we enjoy her cakes and her pies and her elegant vegetable dishes. For just before she left, as a parting gift Mollie gave me copies of all her recipes.

3

Gertie

After Mollie left, our next cook lasted two weeks. A rancher's wife heard we were in need of a cook; she sent Gertie over to see me. Gertie was a thin-faced woman, who wore a faded gingham dress and an apron in need of laundering. Her coal black hair was piled high on her head.

"My namth's Gertie and my manth's namth's Henry," she said, sounding like her mouth was full of moth balls. "My manth's working at the Flying C. The missis over there said you folks needed a cook, so here I am."

Before I could get a word in edgewise, Gertie began telling me her woes. "My manth's got stumik trouble. We got sixth gals and no boys. My manth always wanted a boy. But I told Henry, 'With our sixth gals, your ailin' stumik, my gallstones and floating kidney, you just better forget about a boy.'" She grimaced as though her kidney were floating around somewhere in her anatomy at that very moment.

I had troubles of my own, but I felt sorry for Gertie with

all of hers. I nodded in sympathy and shooed Gertie—gallstones, floating kidney and all—up to the cookhouse. I told her I would join her later.

Poor Gertie! Her whole philosophy of cooking was one of concealment. The place for food was beneath or behind something. You never knew when you might sit down in a dish of cold potatoes or walk knee-deep into a pan of bread dough.

Gertie seemed immune to filth. Flies were everywhere. I bought gallons of bug spray; Gertie never used an ounce. I often wondered if she were not happy living with the flies and mice that had taken command of the cookhouse.

Although one of the cowhands' favorite pies was raisin, they were always doubtful about eating Gertie's. If the raisins didn't crawl, though, they suspected it was safe.

Gertie had only one redeeming characteristic: she was a marvelous cook. If you could shut your eyes to the surrounding filth and not think about what might be hiding in that delicious pie, cake, or pudding you were eating, you could enjoy it.

Not even Pat or Mollie could bake apple pie like Gertie's. The crust was flaky and she demanded we get her fresh apples in season. No canned or dried ones would degrade her pies. It was not only the crust that was good; there was something about the filling that we had never tasted before. Gertie never used spices in her apple pies, and I was determined to learn her secret.

The boys were sworn beef eaters, but there were no complaints when Gertie cooked chicken, especially after they tasted her chicken pies. One of the cowhands told me, "I never thought I'd ever eat so much chicken, but Gertie's is so good I can't seem to get enough of it. One of these days, ma'am, don't you be surprised if you see me out on the range growing wings and trying to fly."

He sighed. "If she just wasn't so damned dirty."

Trouble arose in the bunkhouse while Gertie was working for us. Pat knocked at my door one morning and wouldn't sit down for his usual cup of coffee. By the look on his face, I knew something was wrong.

"Pat, what is it? I know we are in some kind of trouble."

He scratched his bushy gray head in that familiar way of his and confided, "Yes, ma'am." He took a few draws on his pipe. "We sure are. I got my suspicions. I'm thinking we got bugs in the bunkhouse."

"What kind of bugs?"

"Why, bed bugs. I found one in my bunk this mornin'. All the boys been scratchin' somethin' fierce. Now, ma'am, what you goin' to do about it?"

I had always tried to relieve my busy husband, John, of any of the problems that came up at the ranch house. I had even served as peacemaker in the quarrels that came up between the cowhands, or among the cowhands and the cooks. But this might be more than I could cope with.

I left the angel cake I was baking and rushed to the bunkhouse.

I went to Pat's bunk first and turned down his bedroll. Sure enough, Pat was right. Not only were mama and papa bugs scampering about, but so were uncles, aunts, cousins, and a host of friends and neighbors. Their offspring scurried like determined little ghosts, hungry for blood. The older ones looked well fed. I shuddered to think how long they had been feasting on old Pat.

I went to Pete's bunk next. I turned down his bedroll. There, amid another swarm of bugs, I found something equally surprising—a bundle of letters tied together with a piece of twine. I realized the letters were Pete's private property and did not disturb them. But *I* was disturbed by a magazine lying under them in plain view. On the front of the magazine, encircled by a wreath of small, red hearts, was the title, *Lonely Hearts*. I knew the pack of letters must be from a woman in the club.

Quickly, I covered letters and magazine with Pete's

bedroll. If he ever wanted to confide in me, I would be a willing listener. In the meantime, though, that would be his business and none of mine.

At the moment I was more concerned about getting rid of the bugs in the bunkhouse than I was about Pete's love life.

I hunted for John. He was at the corral, just getting ready to drive down to the hayfields. Poor man! He was having enough trouble getting a haying crew together. But I had to tell him about the bugs.

John got out of the ranch truck, wiped the sweat from his brow, released a cuss word or two, and said, "We don't have enough troubles worrying about a dirty cook and a dirty cookhouse. Now we've got to worry about a buggy bunkhouse. I'll see what I can do." As an afterthought he added, "I wonder if they have invaded the cookhouse, too."

"I don't know, but I'll see if I can find out."

I raced to the cookhouse and told Gertie about the bugs. I insisted I have a look at her bed. She didn't seem the least worried about our discovery—I had the feeling it was not an uncommon situation for her—but she was not too pleased with my intrusion. I waded through the dirt and upheaval in her room to examine the bed.

Fortunately, the bugs had not traveled that far.

At the dinner table, I told the crew about the bugs. They all were relieved to know why they had been doing so much scratching lately. Some confessed they had been afraid they might have the seven-year-itch.

John left his work in the hayfields and drove to town, where he asked the druggist how to get rid of the bugs.

Fumigation—that was the answer.

With Pat and Pete's help, John closed all the cracks around the bunkhouse windows, started the fumigation, and shut the door.

The cowhands slept on the new-mown hay in the barn

that night, covering themselves with their horseblankets. Next morning the bunkhouse was aired, the bedrolls taken out on the grass and brushed free of dead bugs. Wholesale murder had been committed. Bedbugs covered the bunkhouse floor.

The bunkhouse was scrubbed clean and left open all day to be aired out by the fresh mountain breeze.

Peace reigned again. I only heard two comments about the experience, one from Pete and another from his counterpart, Pat. "I'd like to take ever'one of 'em bugs," said Pete, "and feed 'em to that so-and-so who brought 'em to us in the first place."

Pat was more philosophical. "Don't suppose the bunkhouse will ever be that clean agin. We better enjoy it while we can. Shure will be good to git a full night's sleep for once."

Although I saw Pete alone several times soon after, he never mentioned the letters or the *Lonely Hearts* magazine. He must have wondered if I saw it. Let him bide his time. I had a feeling that when he was in the right mood he would tell me about them.

Love affairs, especially those of old ranch hands, were none of my concern.

Conditions at the cookhouse did not improve. In fact, they worsened until they reached the stage when we could no longer tolerate them. The mice and flies were in complete control.

Although Pete had not liked Mollie, he disliked Gertie even more. He constantly high-tailed it down to the ranch house to complain about her dirty cooking. One morning he asked if I knew the pan she used to mix up her bread dough. I did; it was the one Pat had used to mix his flapjacks my first morning on the ranch.

"Now, ma'am," Pete said, "Gertie don't use that pan just to mix her bread." I knew Gertie used it for her baking, and I had a sneaking suspicion she used it to soak her feet. But I was ill prepared for what Pat told me next. "This mornin' when I went to the kitchen to get me a drink of cold water, Gertie was jus' a-gettin' up. You know what I saw? I saw her pulling that pan out from under her bed."

We had to let Gertie go back to her "manth."

It hurt me to have to fire her. She didn't seem to resent it, though, and she left in good spirits. As a matter of fact, she was in such a pleasant mood that she gave me all her chicken recipes and revealed the secret flavoring for her mouthwatering apple pies. They were all written in pencil in a little black book, which I later returned.

John agreed to have Pat help me clean out the cookhouse. We did everything from setting mousetraps to emptying a stale slop jar and throwing out moldy biscuits. When the cookhouse was in ship-shape order, all we needed was a cook. That meant it was time for me to go cook hunting again.

4

Jim

Pat told me about Jim, an old roundup cook he knew who lived in a log cabin across the range from the N Bar N. He promised to ask Jim if he would cook for us until we could find a new cook.

I liked Jim the minute I met him. He was the same breed as Pat and Pete. Like them he had spent many years of his life cooking for hungry cowboys on the vast Wyoming ranges. He was happy to help us out in a pinch.

From his appearance I sensed Jim was a gentle and patient man. He was crowned with beautiful white hair. His face was covered with a heavy beard. Its deep lines and weather-beaten skin revealed the years spent on the range. Summer heat and winter blizzards had taken their toll.

During our long conversation, he told me of his early life on the range. His tales were punctuated by belly laughs. "I started shootin' grub for hungry cowhands 'fore I was dry behind the ears. My first job come almost by accident. The J Bar M outfit had shipped 1,600 steers into Wyoming from Nebraska. With all those animals to be branded, their cook, Greasy Ben, got itchy feet and hopped a freight.

"The foreman heard I could cook and offered me fifty dollars a month during roundup. I was only a kid of seventeen, and fifty dollars a month to cook looked like easy money.

"My first night I put the camp in apple-pie order. I dumped a month's supply of grounds from the huge coffee pot and got ready to build the next morning's biscuits. The weavils and rat turds I found in the flour didn't bother me; I jus' sifted them out and went on bakin' my biscuits."

I hired him on the spot.

So long as Jim commanded the cookhouse, the only galloping ulcers the cowboys suffered from were those where their seats and saddles met. He was a good cook, and his disposition was solid gold. But he was a stickler on cookhouse etiquette. Like Mollie he demanded all cowhands deposit their plates in the wreck tub beside the kitchen door. If the first cowboys to eat did not leave fruit pie or pudding for those who drifted in later, Jim just pawed the ground and roared.

And God pity the poor cowboy who sneaked into Jim's pickle barrel!

Many nights after the supper dishes were done Jim walked down to the ranch house and sat on the front steps with me. We watched the moon come up round and gold and mellow. It's light brought out the gentleness of his features.

He told me about his early days cooking and about other cooks he had known. There was Singing Sam, who cooked for years with the old 79 Outfit. As his name implied, Sam was a happy soul. Almost constantly he sang or hummed his favorite tune, "Sweet Rosie O'Grady." The sentimental old cook's most valued possession was a photograph of his lady love, Katie, which he kept always with him in a box.

Jim laughed one of his belly laughs when he told me what happened to Sam one day as the outfit was moving camp. He was driving his chuck wagon over the rocky trail. As it rumbled along, a magpie flew in front of his team—a pair of stubborn mules. The startled mules broke into a run, left the trail, tore across a deep ravine, and upset the wagon. Sam and his crock of sourdough were thrown sky-high and landed on a rocky bank.

The cowboys saw the accident and rode back to Sam's aid. "Are you hurt?" they asked.

"Hurt? I'm dead! Where's my picture of Katie?" He wiped the sourdough from his whiskers and pointed to his empty box. Two of the boys helped Sam up. The others rescued as much sourdough as they could. But nowhere could they find Katie's picture.

Singing Sam cussed every cowboy in the outfit with every cuss word in his vocabulary, coining a few of his own when the standards proved insufficient. The 79 Outfit knew if they did not find Katie's picture Singing Sam would vent his anger on them in more ways than one. Two of the crew rode back on the trail. After a thorough search they found the picture where the wind had blown it into the sagebrush. Katie and Sam were reunited.

As they rode into camp that night, the crew knew Sam was cooking them a good supper. They could smell the steak, cut thick as a wagon tongue. Maybe, just maybe, if he had found a nest of wild turkey eggs and sweet-talked a fresh cow into giving him some milk, there would be custard pie, two inches deep. More important, though, as it floated out to them from the cook tent, was Sam's voice, singing "Sweet Rosie O'Grady."

Another of the many roundup cooks Jim had been acquainted with was known as "Hominy John." John thought the only thing to give his crew the vim and vigor they needed to ride the ranges on a frosty morning was hominy.

When the cowpunchers had eaten so much hominy that

it was ready to come out their ears, they knew they had to act. The next time the ramrod brought camp supplies, they stole the big sack of hominy and threw it in the creek. They laughed and laughed about the way they had duped old Hominy John.

But the trick backfired. Two mornings later when John went to the creek for water, the huge sack of hominy had swollen and floated to the surface. John vowed to feed the outfit hominy until Gabriel blew his horn.

That same evening Jim told me about the barber who had traveled among the camps many years before. One late afternoon the barber rode into camp just as Grumpy George was cooking supper. George flipped a big sack of *something* from his steaming Dutch oven onto the rear of the chuck wagon. The barber asked, "What's *that*?"

"That's son-of-a-bitch-in-a-sack. Ain't you ever et one?"

"No," the barber admitted, "but I've shaved a hell of a lot of 'em."

Another of Jim's tall tales was about Whiskey Joe, an old cook whose sole ambition was to save enough money to buy a barrel of whiskey, jump in, and play "squat and swallow" until the barrel was dry. The boys decided the only way to keep Joe sober and punching the dough was to hide his jug. Several places were suggested—under a bedroll or high in a pine tree or out among the boulders. They finally agreed, however, the perfect place would be in the thorny branches of the buffalo berries.

They had forgotten the old whiskey guzzler had a nose like a hound dog. The next morning his hands were so scratched and sore he couldn't punch his dough, and the cowboys had to go without their biscuits.

Whiskey Joe, though, was better than the cook who next took command of the Dutch oven. Old Jack was not only inebriated ninety percent of the time, he was also dirty—dirtier even than our Gertie. After he had been in camp only a few days the cowhands couldn't stomach the filth.

They agreed unanimously that something had to be done.

That evening after Jack had gone to bed, three of the crew stole into the tent and dragged him from his bedroll. One of them carried a noose. He told Jack if camp wasn't cleaned up he would be wearing it as a necktie.

Then and there Jack decided it was time to hit the breeze, hop a freight, and get the hell out of camp. But before he left he evened the score. Long before daylight, he sneaked out, turned loose all the saddle horses, gathered up all the boys' boots, and filled them with molasses.

Jim told me some of his friends were pretty smart. Pieface Pete not only could bake good pies; he had other talents, too. One day he ran across a broken-down old typewriter. He fiddled with it until he could "pick and peck" one letter at a time.

Pieface Pete turned his newfound skill into a lucrative cow camp business, typing the hands' loveletters for ten cents a page. Many paid Pete for the service, but they insisted he plug his ears when he typed. They'd be damned if he was going to hear anything about their lady loves.

Eventually I felt well enough acquainted with Jim to come right out and ask a question that had long been going through my mind. "Jim, I've wondered many times why you never married. Down through the years didn't you ever fall in love with a girl you wanted to marry?"

Jim didn't answer for a moment, and I knew he was deep in thought. "Wal, I'll tell you ma'am," he said at last, "when I was a young buck, I did give it some thought. I met a good many nice gals in my time. There was one, a schoolmarm, pretty as a picshure. But, hell, I was punchin' cows for fifty dollars a month and found. I wasn't about to get hitched up if I couldn't support my woman. So the years jus' kept passin' me by and I never done it."

For a moment Jim was quiet, and I did not want to disturb his thoughts. Finally he sighed deeply, shook his head, and pulled at the whiskers on his chin. "Oh, hell, ma'am.

COOKIES
PICKLES

Maybe it's fer the best, you know. When I see a man with a good woman and they seem so happy, I think maybe I've missed something all these years. But then again when I see a man married to a hen-peckin' woman and he can't say his soul's his own, wal, then I think maybe I've escaped something."

It took more courage for me to ask the next question. I had often wondered, though, and now was the time to find out. "Jim, maybe it's none of my business, but in all the years you've spent in the West—and you know this is wild country—have you ever been in any kind of trouble? Have you ever been arrested?"

Jim coughed a little, cleared his throat, and chuckled. "Wal, now, I don't mind your askin'. Jus' once when I was cookin' for a big outfit down south I somehow got hold of a beef from another outfit camped near ours. It was all a mistake, ma'am, so help me God. I never did know how that fat critter got into my camp. But when the beef was dressed out I saw the brand and I knowed he wasn't ours." He laughed another of his belly laughs. "You know, ma'am, beef from another ranch always tastes better than your own.

"I was arrested and put in jail. At the trial the lawyer for the other outfit lambasted me good and plenty. He called me every low-down name he could think of, and I felt lower than a rattlesnake's belly. I jus' knowed I was bound for hell sure. Hangin' was too good for a no-good hombre like me.

"But when my lawyer told what a good man I was and all the good things I didn't know I'd done, I knowed I wasn't a cattle thief after all. Guess the judge thought so, too, 'cause he let me go."

One quiet evening when Jim was no longer cooking for us, he walked across the range for one of his welcome visits. One of the boys had shot three fat deer. I invited Jim to stay and have venison stew for supper.

After we ate and Jim had visited with the crew to catch up with news of the ranch, I asked him to walk with me down to the ranch house and enjoy the beauty of the evening. As usual our conversation turned to his early days on the roundup. That night Jim told me the story of his friend Heinie's frightening experience cooking for the Circle C Outfit.

"One day after Heinie had moved camp, he noticed a dressed deer hanging from a cottonwood tree near the cook tent. He had run out of beef, so he thought the boss brought it to tide them over. Heinie made venison stew for supper.

"That night the meat-hungry crew wolfed down the stew. While Heinie cleaned up camp, the boss drove in with the beef. After he deposited the carcass at the chuckwagon, he asked Heinie for something to eat. Heinie dished up a big plate of venison stew from the Dutch oven, and the boss ate it all.

"Suddenly he stopped. 'Say, Heinie, where did you get the stew meat? You told me you were out of beef.'

"'I was,' Heinie answered, 'But I was lucky. I found a dressed deer hangin' on the tree out there.' He pointed it out to the boss. 'I figgered you sent it over, so I cut it down and made this stew. Purty good, ain't it?'

"The boss turned ghostly white and started to shake. 'My God, man, I should have told you. That deer carcass was full of strychnine to poison coyotes!'"

Jim must have noticed my fright. "Don't worry, ma'am, the boss didn't die, and neither did the cowboys. No matter how bad the grub, you can't kill a cowboy."

That old roundup cook with his gentle ways and his chuck wagon quips often made my day. Once just as I walked through the door of the cookhouse, he greeted me with the news that the boys had butchered two fat beeves and brought in their livers. We were having liver and onions for supper, he told me, busily cutting off huge slices of liver. The blood ran through his fingers.

When he stopped cutting and laid down his bloody knife, I sensed he had something special to tell me. "You wanta know something? Ever time I fry liver 'minds me of old Liver Eatin' Johnson. I knowed him many years ago, when I first started cookin' for the old Double Y Bar.

"Ma'am, he jus' pretended to eat them Indian's livers. I 'spect there were times he was mad enough that he could have eaten their livers and maybe the whole Injun. But he never really did.

"I saw him wonst at a carnival in Sheridan. He was using a beef liver to show how he killed them Injuns and ate their livers raw. Two women saw him with that beef liver in his hands and his whiskers and hands a-drippin' blood, and they up and fainted.

"Liver Eatin' Johnson, he was big all over. He wore a number 14 shoe."

Our outfit ate their liver with gusto. But every time I looked at it, all smothered with onions, all I could think about was Liver Eating Johnson with the blood running through his whiskers and over his fingers. I lost my relish for liver quick.

Jim was one of the best cooks ever to flip the lid on a Dutch oven. He told me he would as soon feed his outfit cow chips as the old roundup diet of bacon and beans. He was strictly a lard and butter cook—when he could talk the boss into buying butter. Cowboys from other camps rode large circles to sink their teeth into one of his fruit pies. He always tried his best to get fresh apples for his pies, too; "The bastard who invented dried apples," he said, "ought to be taken out and hanged." But Jim's sarvis berry pies were not very popular. The boys said the purple, juicy berries reminded them too much of bunkhouse bedbugs.

Jim was always on the lookout to cook something new for his crew. When he made macaroni for the first time, the boys looked it over and shied away. It looked too much like grub worms. Jim didn't get by with strawberry gelatin, either. He followed the directions carefully and put the bowl in a cold spring to set. When the boys saw it all red and sparkling they backed away. They'd be damned to eat that "tremblin' bowl of God-knows-what."

Jim was always concerned for the welfare of his boys whose legs were bent to the belly of a horse. Besides cooking for them, he yanked out their aching teeth, treated their snake bites, cured their belly-aches. He often gave them legal advice, and when they confided in him about their love affairs they profited from his sagebrush philosophy.

One August evening Jim was frying chicken at the cookhouse. He turned the crispy, brown pieces in the skillets and sat with me in front of the kitchen door. A cool mountain breeze blew down from the Big Horns. I knew one of his old roundup stories was forthcoming.

"You know, ma'am, ever time I fry chicken, I'm 'minded of the time I cooked for the Double A Bar. We were out of fresh meat. When I come up with a whole Dutch oven full of fried chicken, I s'pose the boys must have wondered where it came from. But they knowed better than to ask. You see, ma'am, we were camped 'side a prairie dog town."

"Jim," I exclaimed, "you didn't!"

He laughed his biggest belly laugh. "Them boys never did know where I got my meat."

Come to think of it, neither did I.

5

Maggie

Jim cooked for us only three months. It got to be too much of an effort for him to arise at 4:30 in the morning and cook for thirty cowhands hungry enough to eat a saddle blanket. His "rumitiz" worsened, his joints swelled, and he couldn't get around. But when he left, he promised to come back and help out in a pinch.

Jim headed back to his little log cabin on the range, and I jumped in my Chevy and headed for the employment agency in Sheridan. I asked the manager if he had a ranch cook for hire.

He did. "Maggie's sitting over there in the corner." He pointed to a middle-aged woman with two large suitcases at her feet. She was skinny as a string bean. "But if you hire her you're stuck with her kid, Willie."

The "kid" looked to be about twelve years old. He was trying to swat a fly with a folded newspaper, pausing to blow a bubble with his gum. As I approached Maggie, the bubble grew and grew until it burst in his face. He scowled at me as though it were my fault.

"Maggie," I began, forcing a friendly smile, "can you cook?"

She jumped from her seat and answered in a high-pitched voice, "Can I cook? Why, ma'am, I can cook a dozen eggs twelve different ways."

Hardly able to hide my disappointment, I remembered once being told a cook was like a book. You can't judge one by its cover. One might look like a saint and prove a she-devil that couldn't boil water. On the other hand, she might look like a hell-raiser and turn out to be an excellent cook and a kind soul. I could only hope for the best.

Desperate enough to hire an orangutan, I offered Maggie the job and reluctantly accepted little Willie, who she called her "baby." I deposited them and their suitcases in the Chevy and headed back to the N Bar N.

During the ride, Maggie spread a wordy blanket over everything I tried to say. I couldn't get a word in edgewise. She seemed to think the world owed her a living, and she was out to get everyone before they could get her. All the while, her twelve-year-old baby blew bubbles in the back seat.

Before Maggie spoke, she always stretched out her neck like a hen getting ready to cackle. At any moment I expected her to squat down on the floor of the car and try to lay an egg. Little Willie, I noticed, had inherited the habit.

I wondered how her behavior would be reflected in her cooking. And I worried about how John and the outfit would react when I arrived with Maggie and her baby at the N Bar N.

My worst fears were realized.

Maggie got off on the wrong foot that night by cooking hash and by baking peach pies without soaking and cooking the dried peaches. If there was anything our bow-legged range riders despised, it was hash. They wanted meat—

steaks sliced thick as a wagon tongue and roasts with rich brown gravy.

From that moment on, our crew disliked Maggie. They practically tore her apart, referring to her bony knees as soupbones and mocking her neck-stretching habit. I defended Maggie. She couldn't help the knees she was born with. And as for her neck-stretching, well, I was certain she couldn't help that either.

Maggie, however, did little to please our outfit. I was certain she cooked food they disliked just for spite. Her cooking depended entirely on her mood. If she were happy and things were going her way, she baked excellent cakes. Her angel food was especially good. The crew called those days, "Happy Grub Days." But there was no name to describe the days she was in her ugly moods. Then I could have bet my best pair of boots that the outfit would be stopping in at my ranch house kitchen—"just for a snack."

Shortly after Maggie arrived, I had to undergo a tonsillectomy. My first day home from the hospital, Maggie rushed down to the ranch house to see me. She had walked far out on the range to pick me a bouquet of wild flowers.

I appreciated her thoughtfulness and thanked her. Throwing the wilted blossoms on the foot of my bed, she looked me over critically. She stretched her neck and clucked, "Gawd Almighty, ma'am, you sure look peaked. I have a niece so puny lookin' just like you. She had her tonsils out, too, and they kept a-growin' back and a-growin' back and a-growin' back! Three times!"

Maggie caught her breath and went on. "Now my Aunt Millie, she's about your size. Course she's lots older. Her tonsils grew big as goose eggs, and after she had them out they just bled and bled and bled. She ain't never been just right since."

Maggie looked me over more critically than before. Her neck stretched one more time. "Well, ma'am, I sure hope you feel better. I got to get a goin'; I'm a cookin' hash for supper, and a big pot of prunes.''

Next to hash, the boys hated prunes more than anything. They dubbed them ''musical fruit.'' For serving the two together Maggie would be lucky if the outfit didn't take her out and string her up.

No sooner had I recovered from my tonsillectomy than Maggie breezed down to the ranch house to ask a favor. ''I'm worried,'' she said, ''that my baby might become a bad boy living here with so many wild cowboys. He is such an innocent little fellow. Would you talk to him and tell him some of the things he should know before the cowboys have a chance to spoil him?''

I agreed to tell Willie about the birds and the bees, so the next morning she sent him down to see me. First I told him to spit out his bubble gum and drink his hot chocolate. Then I asked him a few questions. Then he answered them. I was shocked. Maggie's baby was telling me about sex. I learned more that morning than I had learned in my entire life.

By the time we finished, Maggie need no longer worry about our cowhands polluting her baby's mind. I, however, was concerned about the welfare of the cowhands living around Willie.

The next morning I answered a knock on our front door and came face to face with our good sheriff. He tipped his hat, shook my hand, and explained his visit. ''Now I don't want to frighten you, but a cattle thief escaped from jail last night, and we think he's hiding somewhere on your ranch. If you see any strangers about, please call me.'' He tipped his hat and left.

I hurried to the cookhouse to warn Maggie. She flew into hysterics. ''Where's my baby?'' she screamed.

He was in his usual spot on the cookhouse porch, blowing bubbles and teasing the cat. Maggie ran out, grabbed him by the shoulders, and rushed him inside. As soon as

I left, she braced a chair against the door and lowered all the blinds.

On my way back to the ranch house I scanned the foothills. What I saw in the distance made my heart skip a beat. A stranger! He stood up and stooped down, stood up and stooped down, over and over. What could he be doing? Was he the rustler?

Old Pat was the only one around. I ran to the garden where he was planting potatoes. "Pat," I cried, "the sheriff was just here and told me a cattle rustler had escaped. There's a man acting strangely on top of that foothill. Maybe he's the rustler, or maybe he's just crazy. But will you saddle a horse and ride up there to see what's going on?"

Faithful Old Pat laid down his spade. Without a word of protest he walked to the corral, saddled a horse, and started for the foothills.

I ran to the cookhouse to calm Maggie and tell her what was happening. She paced the kitchen floor, holding little Willie's hand as though the poor kid were going to be snatched from her at any moment. He tried to wriggle out of her grip but could not.

Maggie was raving. She screamed that we would all be murdered. The stranger had the ranch laid out to kill us!

There was a knock at the door.

Maggie screamed her most blood-curdling scream. "He's here! We'll all be killed! Oh, my poor baby!"

I called out, "Who's there?"

We awaited the answer in dread: "It's just Pat, ma'am."

I pulled the chair away from the door and let him in. He sat on it and told us about the man on the foothill. "He wasn't no cattle rustler, ma'am, jus' a poor, lonely sheepherder picking up stones to build a sheepherder's monument to pass the time away."

Always after that, there were days when Maggie kept the

chair braced against the door. We would all have to knock and identify ourselves before she would let us in.

Maggie had several unhappy experiences during her brief stay with us. Two of them involved the outhouses situated side by side among the sagebrush and the thistles.

Early one morning, Maggie visited the cook's privy. Her time inside was brief.

When we heard one of her blood-curdling screams, we all dropped what we were doing and ran out to see what had happened.

Maggie streaked across the sage, trying to hold up her underpants. Her long skinny legs carried her by leaps and bounds through the brush.

"A bear!" she screamed. "A bear! A bear in the backhouse hole bit me!"

I trailed her to her room in the cookhouse and made her lie on the bed so I could examine her recently attacked posterior. There was no sign of a bear's bite but there were plenty of scratches from prickly sage and Russian thistles.

When she insisted there was an animal in the outhouse, however, Maggie was right. Old Pete and two of the younger cowhands headed for the backhouse with their six-shooters. Down in the dark hole, they could discern a furry creature, but they couldn't tell what it was. Whatever it might be, they fired several shots into it. Pete fetched a pitchfork and pulled the body from the hole.

Maggie's bear was an innocent little raccoon. As he eyed the animal's corpse, Pete callously remarked, "Wish it had been a porkypine."

We seldom saw Maggie visit the little house among the sage after that, and we wondered what she did for relief.

Of all the hands at the N Bar N it was Pete who disliked Maggie most. He always tried to annoy her in one way or another. All the disturbances he put in her way were innocent pranks. Some were downright hilarious.

One morning Pete saw Maggie going into the "water

closet,'' as he called it. He picked up several big rocks and rushed with them into the other outhouse.

''Oooohhhhh,'' he groaned horribly. Then he dropped one of the rocks down the hole. He groaned again and dropped another rock. His misery continued until he ran out of ammunition.

Maggie ran to the ranch house to tell me. ''It's Old Pete,'' she cried. ''He's in awful shape. I think you'd better get a doctor right quick.''

Pete had pulled that joke earlier that summer when two young women were visiting us, so I wasn't concerned. I assured Maggie he would recover, but she was still worried when she went back to work.

The state of affairs at the cookhouse went from bad to worse. But whenever Maggie sensed she and her baby might be on their way back to the unemployment agency, she would come up with one of her ''Happy Grub Days.'' Then things would run along smooth as whipped cream.

For some time I had been aware that Maggie had an affliction. She couldn't smell. I kept my knowledge to myself, though, thinking that so far as the outfit was concerned, ignorance was bliss.

One hot July day the boys asked Maggie to make enough ice cream to fill our two five-gallon freezers. It was one of her ''Happy Grub Days,'' so she agreed. Not only that, but she also promised to bake one of her light as a feather angel food cakes, too. Pat hauled the big freezers up from the cave, crushed the ice, mixed it with salt, and froze Maggie's ice cream.

After supper, the outfit was looking forward to sitting on their haunches on the cookhouse porch and lapping up huge bowls of ice cream and cake.

Pete, of course, was first to discover what had happened. He rushed down to the ranch house to tell us, cussing Maggie every step of the way.

Aware of Maggie's affliction, I cringed to think what

might have happened. The time she put sewing machine oil instead of lemon extract in the sponge cake she got away with it. But this time I knew she would not. Maggie, Pete informed us, had flavored the ice cream not with Watkin's vanilla extract, but with a generous dose of Watkin's horse liniment.

I tried to explain the mistake. The bottles looked so much alike and were stored on the same shelf. But I also had to tell the crew Maggie had no sense of smell. After that, nothing I could say or do would appease the men of the N Bar N.

I loaded Maggie, her baby, and their suitcases into my Chevy and drove them back to the employment agency. The manager didn't seem surprised at our appearance.

As I drove back to the ranch I couldn't help but wonder if there were something wrong with me that I was always cook hunting. But what now? There were no other cooks available at the employment agency. Pat was busy working his garden and raising chickens. Jim had gone back to his home on the range. Who was left?

Pete? Perish the thought!

6

Pete, Old Buck, and I

I had good reason to be concerned after Maggie left the N Bar N. It was my destiny to return to the cookhouse and help Old Pete wrangle the pots and pans. While Jim was with us, I had seen little of his friend, Pete. I knew him only through the tricks he played on some of our outfit, and most of them were far from funny. Now it was time to learn more about this stove-up old cowpoke who claimed to have done everything from range riding and bronc breaking to roundup cooking.

The first thing I noticed about Pete was that the trigger finger on his right hand was missing. It was most likely pulled off by a rope when he was breaking a bronc. The second thing I noticed was his tobacco chewing. I never saw him without a cud in one cheek or the other. And when he spat there was no telling where it would land—or when.

"When I gotta spit, I gotta spit," he often reminded me.

I worried about Pete's chewing, especially when he was helping out at the cookhouse. I never found his cud hidden in the mashed potatoes or floating in the gravy, but our little Tommy once found one outside the cookhouse door and ran after me with it in his hand to ask, "What's that?"

Pete's head was large and bald, with just a fringe of black hair that ran from ear to ear. He seemed hale and hearty, which he attributed to cow dung poultices, the fresher the better. He claimed they could do everything from curing gallstones to growing hair on a bald head, though he never was able to explain why the poultices had done nothing to grow hair on his own shining dome.

Pete boasted that he could ride anything that walked on four legs, that he could drink any cowboy under the table, and that he had fathered more offspring than any other man in Wyoming. We took all three claims with a grain of salt.

Soon after Pete started helping at the cookhouse we had a run-in.

Tommy had adored the cowboys from the first day we set foot on the N Bar N. They loved him and gave him their worn-out Stetsons and discarded chaps; I padded the big hats and tried to cut the chaps down to his size. He mimicked their every gesture. When he started picking up their more picturesque figures of speech, though, they tried to muzzle it when he was around.

I had a difficult time once convincing my little cowboy it was not true that if he put horse apples in his pillow and slept on them he would wake a full-fledged cowboy in the morning. I could forgive old Pete for that idea. But the afternoon Tommy ran excited and flushed into the cookhouse kitchen from his play down at the loading chutes to ask, "Mommy, what's a bastard?" I was furious.

It had to be Pete who made that contribution to my son's vocabulary. I confronted him at the loading chutes. "How dare you," I demanded, "use such language around my child?" I braced myself to meet his hair-trigger temper.

But to my surprise he answered in a voice smooth as

cream cheese, "Ma'am, from now on when Tommy is around, I'll try to hobble my tongue."

One day after he was paid his monthly wages, Pete asked me to be his banker. I agreed. Two months I salted away his money.

Like a bolt from the blue he got the "urge" to go to town one Saturday morning. In the twinkling of an eye he had developed the most excruciating pain; in colorful language he showed me its location and described his agony in detail. If I didn't take him to town, he insisted, he wouldn't make it through the day.

Pete demanded his money. I tried to hold back a few dollars, but he wouldn't allow it. He was on a rootin' snootin' spender for sure!

I finally gave him the money and drove him to town in my Chevy, certain that the next time I saw him he would be dead or dead broke.

The boys in our outfit had known of Pete's weakness all along. When they found him paralyzed in a saloon, one of them would bring him home and put him to bed. When he awoke, he was invariably bleary-eyed, broke, and wearing either a skinned nose or a lump on his bald head. Pete never left a saloon without first picking a fight. One night the boys found him standing on a street corner in town, shooting at the moon.

While he was working at the cookhouse he went on a real humdinger. Late the next morning, I decided to run up to the bunkhouse with a bowl of chicken soup and check on him.

One moment I had been in the kitchen making soup and lemon cream pies. The next I found myself in the bunkhouse facing Pete's six-shooter. He was still red-eyed, red-nosed drunk, staggering back and forth, swinging his six-shooter, and swearing energetically.

Two empty whiskey bottles sat on the windowsill. Poor old Pat lay on his bunk with an ulcerated tooth and an ice pack on his jaw. Pete aimed at Pat and laughed idiotically.

''Ma'am, I might as well shoot him and put him out of his misery.'' Pat was in such pain that he groaned and turned the ice pack, not caring if he were shot or not.

I set the bowl of soup on a table and approached the jibbering old cowboy. ''Pete, I know you're just up to one of you're old tricks, but why don't you give me your gun before you accidentally shoot Pat.'' Was that the right approach? Surely I was smart enough to outwit a drunken old cowhand. But Pete just shook his big, bald head. ''Pat's so sick with his tooth,'' I said. ''Don't you think you should stop your fooling around and let him rest?''

Appealing to his better nature was evidently the wrong tactic. ''Now, Ma'am,'' he challenged, pointing his stub finger within an inch of my nose, ''why don't you just try and git my gun?'' He hee-hawed and lunged out of reach.

A button had come off his plaid shirt, and now a tuft of black hair was sticking out like stuffing from a sofa. I knew Pete was just playing, but I *had* to get that gun.

''You're doing good, old girl,'' I assured myself. ''You may get a bullet in your guts or land in a sanitarium, but you're doing just fine.''

Pete had a sweet tooth. I had an idea. ''Pete, I just baked some lemon cream pies. Wouldn't you like to have a piece? You can even have a whole pie.'' He shook his bald head, laughed, and tottered on his boot heels.

One way or another, I had to out-cowboy that old cowboy. ''Pete,'' I whispered, ''if you promise not to tell the boss, I'll get you another bottle. But you'll have to give me the gun first.'' He looked skeptical. Then a loose grin split his face. He staggered over to me, and I led him to the bunkhouse door.

''If you give me your gun, just until you sober up, I'll run to the cookhouse and get you a lemon pie. And if you never tell the boss, I'll give you a bottle.''

Grudgingly, he handed me the gun, and I pushed one

of the empty whiskey bottles from the windowsill into his disappointed hands. "Ma'am, I was only playin' a little joke. That gun ain't loaded; just look and see."

That rip-roaring, gun-toting Calamity Jane might have been more forceful with Pat. But she could have her tactics, and I could have mine. When I left Pete gaping with an empty bottle in exchange for his empty six-shooter... Well, I felt I had handled the situation admirably.

It was several days before I gave the gun back to Pete. He never asked me for it, and when I gave it to him he didn't say a word. He just bowlegged back to the bunkhouse with it.

Not too long after that, Pete knocked at my kitchen door. He took off his big hat to reveal his shining dome and doodled his Adam's apple a few doodles. "Ma'am, how would you like to ride over to the lake pasture with me? It sure would be a nice jaunt on a sunny morning like this. I'll go screw a saddle on a pony for you and bring him up to the hitching post."

How nice it was for Pete so quickly to forget the fracas at the bunkhouse. "Pete, it's kind of you to ask, but I've never been on a horse in my life."

"That so? Wal, we just gotta do something about that!" He grinned at me foolishly and seemed pleased he was to be my first teacher.

Why shouldn't I ride? I wasn't old or corpulent or rheumatic. I was smart enough. Everyone at the ranch rode. Even little Tommy had his own mount. Horse-happy, I raced to my bedroom. I donned a pair of jeans and a western shirt and pulled on my new boots.

Pete came back leading Buck, an enormous, bony, big-framed beast with a head like a hammer and a neck like a moose. He had blood in his eye and took an immediate dislike to me. He was no pony, but I had come prepared. I took a lump of sugar from my pocket and gingerly held it to his mouth.

Buck shook his head and blew slobbers in my face. "I don't think he likes me," I said. "I think he's going to kick me."

"Now, Ma'am, don't be skittish. He don't kick from that end. You and Buck will get along just fine once he gets to know you a little better."

I said, "Nice horsey, nice horsey," and patted Buck's bony backside. He crooked his neck and rolled his eyes from side to side. His expression said, "Just wait, old girl, until I get you on my back!"

Pete helped me clamber up into the saddle, where I sat like a sack of cement. Then with one swing of his long leg, Pete was mounted. Without a word, he motioned for me to follow, spurred his horse, and was off for the great open spaces.

I had only a moment to ask myself if I were supposed to follow at the same break-neck speed before Buck threw up his tail and leaped like a gazelle. I was sitting on a cushion of air, only to descend with great force onto the animal's neck. I would ride that big brute if it killed me.

I called to Pete for help, but if he heard me he paid no attention. He put the spurs to his horse and galloped off without looking back. Was this his vengeance for my taking away his gun? I was angry and confused. "If I live to get back to the ranch, I'll kill him. I'll kill him and good riddance! I'll have that old whiskey guzzler fired!"

At the moment, though, it was more important to concentrate on staying on Old Buck than to plan my revenge on Old Pete. The old outlaw jumped irrigation ditches. He sped across ranges. He dodged huge boulders.

Hairpinned to Old Buck's side, I hung on to the saddle horn for dear life. When we reached the lake pasture I knew Pete would stop, get off his horse, ask me how I was doing and apologize. I was wrong. Without a word, he turned his horse around on two legs, and galloped back to the N Bar N lickety-split.

Only through sheer anger did I survive the ride back with Old Buck running like crazy, his lungs blowing like bellows. When we reached the corral, Buck stopped in his tracks. I kept going. I picked myself up off the ground, threw away a handful of Buck's mane, and stuffed my shirt back into my jeans.

Pete, the old booze hound, was walking toward me. I was primed to chew him up good, to call him every vile name I had learned from the cowboy's vocabulary. I wanted his old bald head out of my sight forever. He could just take his lousy bedroll and get out. I would have told him so, too, but I was too tired and bruised, so I just screamed at him to keep his distance. My feet crying for release from the new boots, I crawled angrily back to the ranch house.

I learned many things about the whang-leathered old cowboy that day. Affection was not one of them. Would there be more times that he would try to get me in a tight place and turn on the heat? I would long remember the day.

It was dear old Jim who later found me sitting on the back porch, trying to pull the new boots from my feet. I couldn't hold back the tears. I told Jim how Pete had left me to do or die. Jim let me vent my anger and then finally said, "I think the old devil likes you, ma'am. He's jus' got a poor way a showin' it. I've known him for many, many years, and I can tell you he only hurts the ones he loves. You jus' dry them purty blue eyes and don't go ridin' with the damned fool no more."

He pointed to the corral. "And don't feel bad that you and Old Buck didn't get along. He's thrown two of the boys already. You done real, real good jus' to stay on his back."

I knew he was trying to build up my spirits. "Now, ma'am, ain't nothin' worse than breakin' in a new pair of boots. In the mornin' I'll fill 'em full of oats and water. When them oats starts to swell they'll stretch hell out of them boots."

He took a firm grip on one of my boots and bent over

in front of me. "Now you just push against my backside with your other foot, and we'll have this boot off before you can say 'scat.' You just gotta have a boot jack. A wooden one. Them metal boot jacks ain't no good."

I asked Jim to stay for supper, but he said he had to "git a-goin'." Early the next morning I learned why he was in such a hurry. He presented me with a fine wooden bootjack that he must have stayed up all night to make. Tacked to it was a message scribbled on a piece of brown paper: "Mam, scuze my spellin this pensel don't spell worth a dam. Dont you wury bout them new boots no more. they's goin to be fine. Iv helped bury many a cowboy with his boots on, but nary a gal.—Jim."

7

Bessie

Although I had told Jim I would never help Pete in the cookhouse again, I was forced to eat crow. One of the busiest times at the ranch came when the outfit laid down their saddles to help put up the huge quantity of hay needed to feed the thousands of cattle on a ranch as large as ours. I had to help with the cooking, so when a dry-land farmer drove into the ranch one day and asked if we needed a cook, I snapped up the opportunity.

The farmer said a woman in need of a job was living with him and his family. From the tone of his voice, I sensed she had worn out her welcome. As soon as I had a chance, I jumped in my Chevy and high-tailed it to the dry-land range to hire Bessie.

She had been expecting me and was wearing an astonishing green dress that had seen its better days. It was spruced up with a bright red sash tied in an enormous bow at the back. Bobbing crazily up and down on her head was a tiny red hat with an enormous purple feather. All in all she was dressed to kill.

Her suitcase bulged at the seams. It, too, had known better times.

Bessie's pathetic, slightly cock-eyed appearance did not necessarily mean she couldn't cook. I decided she should be given a chance. But I was concerned about the reaction we would get from the boys when I deposited her at the cookhouse. Whenever I hired a new cook, their expectations ran high. They wanted a pretty lady, a sexy woman, and a good cook all wrapped up into one package.

I loaded Bessie and her suitcase in the Chevy and took off for the N Bar N. During the drive she pumped me with questions.

"How many cowboys work at the ranch?"

"We have about thirty regular hands."

"Are any of them married?"

"They're all single."

"How old are they?"

"Some are young, some are older."

She smiled and settled down in her seat. I was concerned with all her questions. Was she coming to the N Bar N to cook or to catch a man?

Old Pete watched us drive into the ranch. As I waited in the car for Bessie to get out her suitcase, he stuck his bald head in the window and pointed his stub finger at her. "Ma'am," he demanded, "where did you ever find *that*?"

Once I got Bessie settled in the cookhouse and explained her duties, I stayed out of sight until the boys had a chance to recover from the shock. She turned out to be a Dr. Jekyl and Mr. Hyde, and her cooking reflected her moods. A meal cooked on one of her bad days could put the N Bar N outfit out of commission for a week. Only later did I learn what caused those changes of mood.

Bessie was not popular among our hands, but Hank, one of the newer cowboys, disliked her the most. Hank wore a bridgework of six false teeth. For some reason he always took it out and set it beside his plate before he ate.

One morning after breakfast Hank forgot to pick up his teeth. He rushed back to the cookhouse to retrieve them, but they were already gone. Bessie must have brushed them in with the scraps when she cleared the table, but Hank accused her of stealing them.

"What would I want with the damned things?" she asked him. "I have teeth of my own." After that, every time Bessie dressed a chicken Hank insisted she save the entrails so he could look for his teeth.

Seldom did any of the boys stay long at the cookhouse, and never did they go there alone. Finally I asked one of the younger cowboys why Bessie was so unpopular. "She's a manchaser, ma'am," he told me. "She'd take the clothes right off of you, pants and all."

I explained that Bessie didn't mean anything by her amorous pursuit. She was just lonely, and it would be a nice gesture if the boys would be a little kinder to her. His only answer as he walked out the door was, "Ha. Ha. Ha."

More concerned than ever, I decided to get at the root of the problem by asking Old Pat, but not even he could help. "That woman is lovesick," he said. "A man would have to be hard up to give her a second look."

Now I worried how far Bessie would go to hook one of our boys. Like a mother hen, I didn't want any of them getting into trouble. I had no choice but to let Bessie go. As gently as I could, I told her we no longer needed her. To soften the blow I added that I might have to do the cooking myself; at the moment that was more truth than fiction. "I'll give you two weeks pay, and you'll have enough money to go back to South Dakota."

She wailed into the beef stew simmering on the stove. "I don't want to go back to South Dakota!"

I would have to be firm. A bribe might help. "Bessie,

I'll tell you what: I'll give you that white hat of mine that you like so much.''

''I don't want to go!''

There was nothing I could do but shut the door on her wailing and hope for the best.

As far as I could determine, Bessie left our crew unscathed, but that was not the last we heard of her. One afternoon an old cowhand from South Dakota came to the ranch. He rode the grubline a few days and exchanged gossip about the females with our crew.

When the boys told the old cowhand about Bessie, he recounted a long, drawn-out history of her past in South Dakota. She was out to get a man any way she could, all right, but she was not the country bumpkin we had thought. She had been married, in order, to a butcher, a plumber, a baker, and a dry-land farmer. After a few months of marriage, each had sent her packing.

Poor Bessie! I've often wondered if she ever caught her man.

8

Pete's Ghost and the Mountain Oysters

Bessie left during branding, a time when good cooks are hard to find. I had no luck replacing her. So, although no woman in her right mind would have done it, I found myself back at the cookhouse helping Pete. I was determined to ignore his tobacco chewing and other annoying habits.

Pete seemed hale and hearty to me, but he often complained he was "bound up" and would wheedle me for cathartics. If anyone else were present, he would call me aside and whisper loudly, "Ma'am, I need another physic. Do you have one that don't gripe? That castor oil you gave me yesterday jus' griped the hell outa me."

"Namonya," I learned, ran in Pete's family. It got Old Uncle Gus, and Pete knew it would only be a matter of time before it got him, too.

While I was helping Pete cook, John bought a large cream separator. Until then, when Pat brought in his big buckets of milk, we had gone through the long process of straining it, pouring it into crocks, and placing it in the cooler to wait for the cream to rise. Then we could finally skim the cream off the top. Now, all Pat had to do was turn the crank and sweet cream would come out one spout and skim milk out the other.

Most the boys were only mildly interested in the separator, but Pete was fascinated with it. I had to ask him why. "Well, ma'am," he said, "I'll tell you. Saturday night in the saloon an old cowboy told me if I run antifreeze through the separator I can drink what comes out the cream spout."

During the month that I helped Pete at the cookhouse, he saw a ghost. And he swore he had not been drinking. Someone had been sneaking into our big lake pasture and cutting the fences to make it open grazing for another cattle outfit. John was determined to find out who. He had Pete ride out and keep watch at night.

One morning Pete returned tired and bleary-eyed. At breakfast he told us about the ghost. Yessir, he was riding fence when it rose right up out of the ground and chased him!

Pete was not about to return to that lake pasture. The boss would just have to get somebody else to play Sherlock Holmes. We all took Pete's tale with a grain of salt. It was probably just another of his whiskey dreams. But when he insisted it was true we decided something really must have scared him.

Jack, a cowboy who claimed he wasn't afraid of a ghost or anything else, volunteered to keep watch that night. Pete's ghost made for interesting conversation the rest of the day, and we all looked forward to Jack's report.

We didn't see Jack until late the next morning. Had he caught the person cutting our fences? More importantly, had he seen the ghost?

"Yes," Jack announced. "I saw it." The spectre had risen

out of the sage and chased him, just as Pete said. "I saw it, all right, but it had four legs and a tail."

"Legs and a tail?" We were all puzzled.

"Yes, and a mane."

"You mean?" Now we knew.

"A cow pony with a white neck and head. He was grazing inside the fence, and when he saw another horse run by he raised up and ran along."

We could all stop worrying about Pete's ghost. The only spirits we need worry about were those confined in his bottle.

With all the activity of branding time, Pete and I needed more help, so Pat agreed to let his job wrangling hens go for awhile. We were all three working at white heat when Pete pulled another of his tricks on me.

The first day of branding Pat and Pete offered to prepare the rest of the food if I would bake the huge beef roasts and make the mashed potatoes and gravy. Pat would cook vegetables from his garden, and Pete would bake the pies.

Early that afternoon, Pete bow-legged down to the corrals where the boys were branding. He returned toting two huge buckets. They were full of mountain oysters, he said. He was going to fry them for supper. I was busy at the time and gave it no thought.

As the branding crew ambled up to the cookhouse to wash for supper, I sliced huge pieces of tender roast beef, mashed mountains of potatoes with sweet cream and ranch butter, and filled bowls with rich brown gravy.

Pete busied himself filling the huge iron skillets with lard. When it was hot he dropped in the oysters one after another. He had covered them with a coating of some sort. They sizzled and fried and smelled tantalizing.

When we sat down, the cowhands heaped their plates with roast, potatoes, and vegetables, but all seemed to prefer the fried oysters. Pete urged me to eat some. I tried one. It was so good I ate another and another and another.

Later, while Pat and I were putting away the leftovers, I started wondering about those oysters. I had always either scalloped oysters or made stew with them. "Pat, where did Pete come up with oysters this time of year? The only time I could buy them back in Iowa was at Thanksgiving or Christmas. Is 'Mountain' a new brand?"

If I had smacked Old Pat in the kisser he could not have looked more surprised. "You mean you don't know about them oysters?"

"No. Where did Pete come up with them so suddenly?"

Pat was skeptical. "Hasn't the boss ever told you where mountain oysters come from?" He thought for a moment, and I could see he was getting angry. "That damned old Pete must have known. Now I know why he kept insistin' you eat more of 'em."

I assured Pat they were delicious, but I was beginning to have my doubts. "What's all the hubbub about?"

"Guess it's up to me to tell you." He hemmed and hawed, then cleared his throat.

"You know, ma'am, we branded five hundred calves today?" I nodded, but I still didn't see what that had to do with the oysters. Had this old roundup cook suddenly lost his marbles?

"Well, ma'am," he stammered, "we castrated 'em, too."

I looked at Pat and then over at the stove where the huge skillets waited to be put away. When I realized what I had just eaten—and with relish—my stomach rebelled. As fast as I could, I ran out the cookhouse door.

The episode of the mountain oysters was soon overshadowed by an accident. I fell off the cookhouse steps, badly spraining my ankle. For over an hour I couldn't move. When Pat and Pete finally found me, they carried me down to the ranch house and put me to bed. When John returned from town with ranch supplies, he called our good doctor immediately.

During my recovery, all the attention I received from the

boys at the N Bar N made me almost glad I had been injured. My dressing table was crammed with sacks of jelly beans, boxes of chocolates, packages of chewing gum, frosty bottles of pop, and pitchers of ice-cold lemonade. Bouquets of wild flowers were carried miles on the backs of cow ponies. They were a beautiful expression of affection, even though they were wilted.

Newly purchased pairs of chaps and boots were brought to my room and displayed for my approval. Picture albums were placed on my knees, each photo explained and chuckled over.

Old Pat spent hours at my bedside delivering all the news about the N Bar N. He and Pete and the cooking were getting along just fine, he assured me. I often had my doubts, but I could only hope for the best.

I was never allowed to go hungry. Pat brought me breasts of prairie chicken fried in sweet butter and fresh vegetables prepared with infinite trouble and care.

Not to be outdone, Old Pete often came down to see me. Although I looked forward to his visits, I never knew what he might say or do. Early one morning he dropped in to give me some of his sagebrush advice. He sat down on a chair near my bed. After looking me over for a minute, he shook his big bald head and said, "Ma'am, you're damned lucky you didn't break that leg. In Wyoming when a female breaks her leg we figger she ain't no more good than a lame cow pony, so we jus' take her out and shoot her." He laughed heartily, expecting me to do the same. At the moment, however, his joke was as funny as a kick in the pants.

Every day Pete bow-legged down to see me, holding a plate of something he had cooked especially for me. A dish towel folded across one arm, he inevitably bowed like a snooty waiter before presenting the dish. "Ma'am, I shot this grouse yisterday, dressed her out, and cooked her special fer you.'' He set down the bird and continued. ''And I'm a-bakin' fresh bread fer your supper.''

I had once seen Pete dress a grouse. By the time he finished, neither he nor the bird smelled very appetizing. I had witnessed his bread-baking, too. He put all his energy into kneading the dough. When it was at last kneaded to his satisfaction, he planked it down on the table and finished by rubbing all the remaining dough off his arms and hands and kneading it back into the huge mound. I had to wonder how many long black hairs from Pete's arms went into the bread and how well it was seasoned with heifer dust.

In times like this, Pete and Pat and the rest of the boys blew to smithereens the old saying that a cowboy thinks more of his pony than he does of a woman.

9

Pete's Model T

The branding ended, my ankle healed, and I returned to the cookhouse. I was still determined to find a new cook, but until I did I would be stuck with my job helping Pete. At last I reached the stage that I thought I knew what made Old Pete tick, but I was not prepared for the announcement he made one morning after breakfast. The outfit had left the table, and he and I were sitting down for a second cup of coffee. "Yup, I bet you can't guess what I done yisterday."

Before I had time to guess, he blurted out the answer. "I done bought myself a autymobile. A open-faced Model T. Course, it ain't as new and fancy as your Chevy, but it runs. I never owned a autymobile before, but I jus' decided I'm not a-goin' to bother you nor the boys to take me to town ever Saturday night. And I'm not a-goin' to ride that old horse of mine to town one more time."

Pete paused a long time to drink coffee. He was giving the news plenty of time to sink in before he continued. "Don't s'pose you could learn me how to drive?" When

I didn't answer, he added, "You know, ma'am, I'll jus' have a hell of a time to make her go if you don't help me get started."

"Pete," I said, "You ought to have your head examined." Why should I do him any favors after all the tricks he had played on me? He looked so hurt and disappointed waiting for my answer, though, that I weakened. Too, I could hear Jim telling me Pete only hurt the ones he loved, and I heard myself saying, "Pete, I'm sure the Model T will only breed disaster. But I'll try to find time to teach you. I only hope I can do the impossible."

"I jus' knowed you would! Now I'm going to have a autymobile like the rest of the young bucks." He wiped the coffee from his mouth with his sleeve and thoughtfully leaned one hand on his chin. "My car's settin' back of the bunkhouse right now. Do you think we could take a ride first thing tomorrow mornin'?"

I still thought Pete had gone off his rocker buying the old Ford. And I knew I was getting too involved.

Before I could brush the sleep from my eyes the next morning, Pete knocked at the kitchen door. "I've fixed the boys' breakfast and done all the dishes and I'm ready to go." Not too impatiently, he waited until I had finished my breakfast and joined me in a second cup of coffee.

The car was of an even more ancient vintage than I had expected. Pete refused to tell me what he had paid for it. But whatever the amount, it was far too much. I took the crank and tried to start the motor. The old Ford refused. It didn't even burp. It would take more than two cups of coffee to awaken this ancient wreckage.

"Now, ma'am, you jus' show me how to start the damned thing and show me what makes her go and we'll git a-goin'." I tried to turn the crank again, then turned it over to Pete. He gave it a wild turn in the Model T's belly. The old car coughed twice, palsied for a minute, then convulsed to a stop.

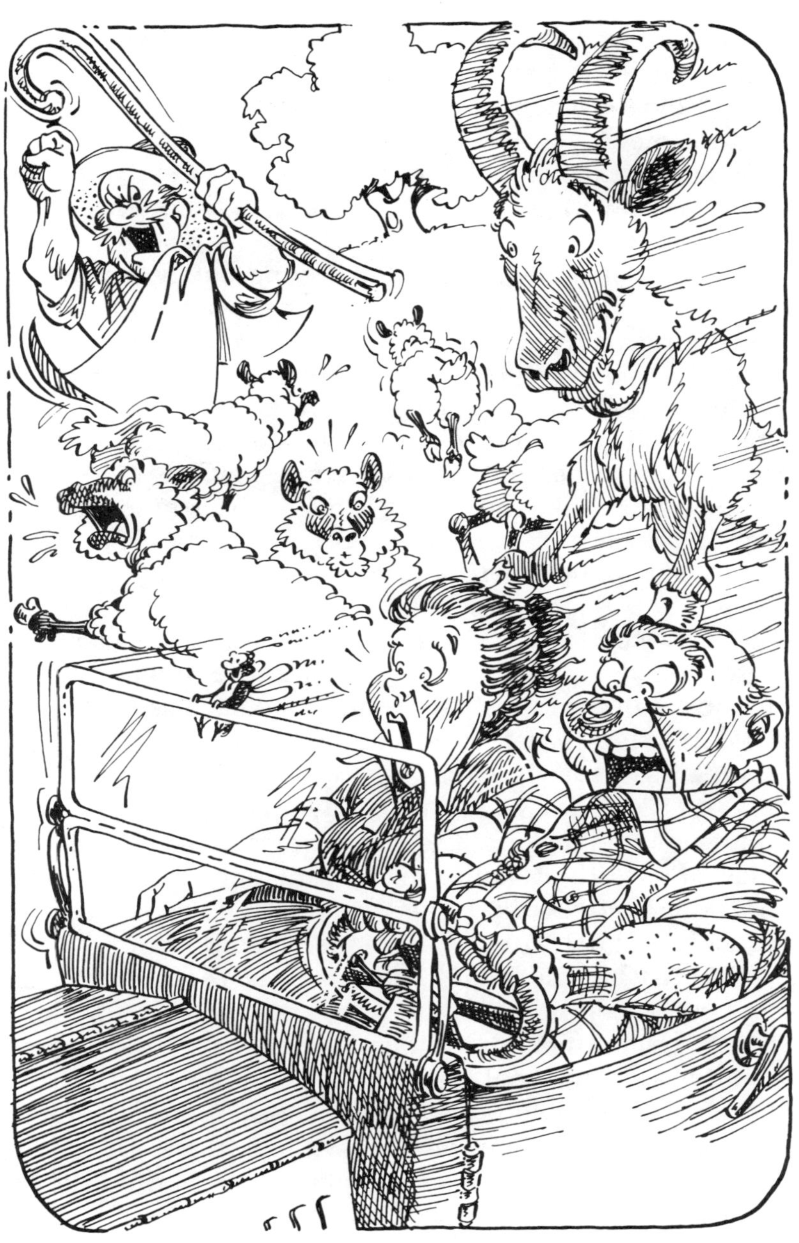

Pete cranked three more times before it sputtered to life, fueled by a flow of profanity.

The old Ford bounced, and Pete and I jumped in. I was at the wheel.

As we bucked along down the road, Pete's spirits hit an all time low. "Our old nags can trot faster than this autymobile," he moaned.

I tried to encourage him. "I'm driving slowly so you can watch me. I'll drive a few miles, turn the car around, and you can drive back." Pete grimly agreed.

We passed Pat on his way to the mailbox. I gaily invited him to jump on the running board. He shook his bushy white head and called back that life was still good to him; he wanted to hang on to his a while longer.

As soon as I had the Model T headed back to the ranch, I pulled over and exchanged seats with Pete. He took a death grip on the steering wheel and glued his eyes to the road.

We rounded a turn in the road to find ourselves headed into a band of sheep entering the highway on their way to the mountain range. I screamed at Pete to use the brake. "I don't know where it is!" he yelled back and stomped on the gas pedal instead.

With Pete yelling, "Whoa, damn you, whoa!" we plunged into the flock. The sheepherder shook his fist and blasted us with profanity. After hitting an old ewe in the backside, Pete bodily pulled me into the driver's seat. I squeezed under him and took the wheel.

Pete gnashed his teeth. "There oughta be a law agin them damned sheep bein' on the road. Stop my car 'fore any more of 'em run into us. If them Democrats in Washington don't pass a law 'bout these sheep on the road, by Gawd, I'll change my polytics." I had never seen him so angry.

I turned off the ignition. "Now, Pete, there's no other way to get the sheep to the mountains." That did little to console him.

He spit a stream of tobacco juice at an old buck nosing around the hood. "Maybe you're right, but I hope the outfit that owns this band of woollies gets nothin' but singles come lambin' time." It was half an hour before I could edge the old Ford through the thousands of bleating sheep. All the while Pete lambasted them, not missing a single one.

When he had finally calmed down, I persuaded him to take the wheel again. "The only way you'll ever learn to drive your Ford, Pete, is to keep on driving." Reluctantly, he slid back into the driver's seat. I hugged the passenger's seat with both hands, and away we chugged. Somehow Pete managed to dodge the fences and I managed to dodge his judicial squirts of tobacco juice.

We hurtled the rest of the way back to the N Bar N. Pete turned into the driveway on two wheels, just missing a six-foot ditch and the mailbox.

Eventually Pete learned to drive his Model T, at least to his own satisfaction. I was the only one in our outfit who had the courage to ride with him. The "autymobile" always stopped so suddenly that I nearly flew into the motor, and Pete never kept both hands on the wheel. He always had to point something out to me. When I warned him against his practice of driving on the wrong side of the road, he simply insisted he liked that side better.

The old cowboy ran his Model T mostly on cheap gasoline and faith. It was almost always low on oil and water. But if I reminded Pete of those necessities, he reminded me back that it was "still a-runnin'."

Whenever we returned from a ride, Pete took the driveway on two wheels and jerked to a halt. Then he would remove his lanky old body from behind the wheel, scratch his big bald head, and announce, "Wal, we made it." Solely by an act of Providence, we had.

One Sunday morning I found Pete greasing the old Ford with a mixture of crude oil and flour. He was quick to inform me that the Forty-niners had used the concoction to grease their covered wagons. ''Their wheels rolled on it clear to Californy.'' With treatment like that, Pete's Model T rarely ran. Most of the time it sat behind the bunkhouse, rusty, lazy, and sleepy.

10

Chuck

In the midst of haying season we still were without a cook. One Tuesday afternoon as I took a breather at the ranch house, I was startled by a loud knock at the kitchen door.

Opening the door, I found myself face to face with a huge, beefy brute. His appearance frightened me. He had a head of bushy black hair, a bullish neck, and a scornful expression.

"Do you need a cook?" he demanded.

"Yes, we do. Are you applying?"

"Do I get the job?"

I hesitated. "What's your name?"

"Chuck."

"Chuck who?"

"Just Chuck."

Despite his appearance and his refusal to tell me his last name, I was determined to hire a cook. Chuck got the job.

On the cookhouse porch Tommy's cat was sunning himself. Chuck went out of his way to kick him viciously with his boot. The poor animal landed in a clump of sage, where he mewed pitifully and licked his wounds. Chuck's only comment was matter of fact. "Never did like cats."

Eventually Chuck had to give John his last name to get on the payroll. But we were never sure if it was really Jones.

Chuck told me he had been the head chef at the Waldorf Astoria Hotel in New York City for five years. He did not say why he left. But the first meal he cooked for the N Bar N was never to be forgotten. There were no limits to the thick cream, ranch butter, garden vegetables, and prime meat.

The gourmet meals Chuck set on the table at our cookhouse left no doubt that he was at least telling the truth about having cooked at the Waldorf. He served dishes we had never heard of, with names we could not pronounce. He knew of ways to prepare beef other than as steaks or roasts. Eggplant souffle, breakfast hash, and chocolate rice were just a few of the delicious treats he served up.

Who ever heard of French cuisine being served in the cookhouse of a Wyoming cattle ranch? Our hands let it be known all over the cattle country that we had a cook from the Waldorf. Word soon spread that it wasn't necessary to spend a fortune in New York City to enjoy a meal fit for a king. The finest international dining could be experienced for free, just by dropping in at the N Bar N. While Chuck was with us we had more visitors stop in at the ranch than we had ever had before. And, under one pretense or another, they always managed to arrive right a mealtime.

While Chuck was with us, Pete took a summer cold that would not improve. The congestion settled in his chest, and he was forced to stay on his bunk. When I was told our doctor was on a fishing trip, I called on an old ranch woman for advice.

"There's nothing like a mustard plaster for a cold on the chest," she told me. "I've cured many a cowboy with one. Just use plenty of mustard."

With Jack and two of our strongest cowboys holding Pete down, I applied the plaster. Pete squirmed in his bunk, yelling at me to "take that damned burning thing off!" First he cussed the boys for holding him down. Then he cussed everyone at the N Bar N in general.

I was convinced that the longer the plaster stayed on Pete's chest the better. A half hour would be ideal. When the time was up, I peeled the plaster off. Pete's tough old hide came off right along with it.

Our old booze hound recovered from his cold in spite of my care. Later Pat and I discussed the severity of the illness. "You know, ma'am," Pat told me quite seriously, "Old Pete woulda never made it if he hadn't had such a strong constipation."

Regardless of Chuck's genious in the kitchen, something about him gave me the squirms. It finally reached the stage that I was actually afraid of him. He always kept his array of butcher knives razor sharp and often slashed out at anything within reach.

Chuck never allowed Pat to catch the chickens he butchered. As Pat had raised them since the day they began to peep, he felt he should have a say in their demise and resented the intrusion. But he decided not to argue with the brutal-looking chef who had taken complete charge of the cookhouse.

One Sunday morning I saw Chuck catching chickens for dinner. He grabbed several fat hens in each of his huge hands and ran with them to the cookhouse. They squawked and tried to escape, but to no avail. He threw one on the ground, put his enormous foot on her head, and pulled at her neck until she was decapitated. He discarded the bleeding body in the dirt, grabbed another hen, and killed her in the same cruel way.

I told John what I had witnessed. I was terrified. "The way Chuck tore the heads off those chickens, heaven only knows what he could do to ours. French cooking or not,

I can't stand having him around any longer. I'll admit I hired him, John, but you'll have to fire him. Get rid of him, but don't antagonize him. Tell him the company's going broke, tell him we're selling off the cattle, tell him the cowhands have mutinied. Tell him anything!"

To this day I don't know what John actually told Chuck. Before he left, however, I wasn't so afraid of the brute that I didn't sneak up to the cookhouse and steal some of his recipes.

11

Etta

I was beginning to think all the mean and disagreeable cooks in the world somehow landed at the cookhouse at the N Bar N. Pete was itching to get back in the saddle and I was climbing the cookhouse walls when I finally heard about a schoolteacher who was looking for a summer job. I just might sweet talk her into cooking for our outfit.

Once more I drove to town. After visiting with Etta for a few minutes, I hoped she might work out. At least I would get a much needed rest and Pete would get his boots back in the stirrups. So Etta was the next cook to flip a dishrag at the N Bar N.

The cowboys were dubious when I told them our new cook was a schoolteacher. She had been a high school teacher in Iowa, I explained, and might be a good cook in spite of it. Her intelligence in the schoolroom might even carry over to the kitchen. But when I deposited her at the cookhouse with her library of encyclopedias and textbooks, I made sure they were packed away out of sight in her bedroom.

Immediately, the outfit wanted to know if she were pretty. I hemmed and hawed and finally said, "Let's just say she is different. But I'm hiring Etta to cook, not to enter a beauty contest." The truth was that Etta was a middle-aged, straight-laced, old-fashioned schoolma'am. She wore large spectacles and kept her hair drawn tightly back in a bun. I held to the faith, however, that sooner or later I would hit the jackpot; maybe Etta would surprise us.

She did.

I told her that our last cook had been a chef at the Waldorf. I did not expect her to follow in his footsteps, but I did emphasize the fact that our cowhands liked filling food—meat and potatoes, macaroni and cheese, pies, cakes, and puddings. Above all, they demanded good bread.

Etta's bread? The boys could not eat it. I suggested she try biscuits. They, too, were a disaster. The first time I saw them solidly piled in the cookhouse oven, I thought the dough had aborted. They were hard and flat. To keep peace at the cookhouse, John finally drove to town and bought store bread, which the cowboys despised. They called it "gum waddin'."

Etta, however, did bake delicious pies. They were culinary miracles. One day she informed me that she was going to make mincemeat for pies. Pat overheard our conversation and told us, "There's no damn sense in making mincemeat when there's gallons of it in the cave. I'll go get some."

In a few minutes Pat was back, but had no mincemeat. "You can't use that mincemeat, ma'am. It's stronger'n me and has bubbled all outa the crocks. Maybe the chickens'll like it." That proved to be an understatement.

The next morning Pat dropped by my kitchen to "chew a little fat" and have his usual cup of coffee. He took a few puffs on his corncob pipe, laid it on the kitchen table, and laughed out loud. I asked what was so funny.

"You won't believe it, ma'am. You know that mincemeat that was in the cave?" I nodded. "Wal, I cleaned out the crocks an' took it all bubblin' down to the chicken yard. Them chickens of mine gobbled it up, and they all got drunk. My old roosters are staggering all over the chicken yard, and them old hens that ain't laid for months are just a-settin' and a-strugglin'."

When Pat noticed my skepticism, he made me go see for myself. I was convinced he was exaggerating, but when I reached the chicken yard and saw Pat's chickens I couldn't believe my eyes. They were just plain drunk. "Wal, ma'am, all I can say is that mincemeat had a hell of a lot of brandy. Didja ever see anything like it?"

"Yes, Pat, I have—when Pete comes home on a Saturday night."

While Etta cooked for us, Pat had trouble eating. It was due partly to her cooking, but mostly to his teeth. Long ago he had promised to do something about those old snags of his. Many nights he went to bed with an ice pack on a jaw swollen with an infected tooth. At last he went to the dentist, and when he came back, he told us he would have to have his teeth pulled. Sadly he said, "The doc says I got gonorrhea of the gumes." How Pat could mutilate the English language!

Because of Pat's age, the dentist pulled only a few teeth at a time. Until they were all out and his mouth was healed, I kept him supplied with custard and comfort.

With their blood-red gums and bits of white enamel, Pat's dentures looked ghoulish. It was a trying time for us all when he tried to break them in. His cursing was more poignant than I had ever heard it. Several times a day he would burst into my kitchen. He removed the bits of crockery from behind his gray beard. He wiped off the remains of his last meal with his red bandana. Then he would

thrust the dentures under my nose and explain in detail what was wrong with each individual tooth.

"Now, Ma'am, you see this here one?" He pointed it out to me. "It rubs aginst my gume way back in here." He would open his toothless mouth and point to the exact spot. "Now it's sore as hell. That tooth has sure got it in fer me."

Then he would motion for me to come closer so he could show me another one. "Jus' look at this one on t'other side. It hangs on to ever' thing I eat and won't let go when I try to swaller. An' that one right above jus' goes up and down, up and down, up and down when I try to chew.

"Now these in front, they bite like a bulldog. Don't my tongue look red to you? Don't it look like it's been bit?" He stuck his tongue out for me to look.

When he finished his discourse, he dried his dentures on the seat of his pants and tucked them safely beside the sack of Bull Durham in his vest pocket. Away he went to the bunkhouse, cussing every step of the way.

Every time Pat bit down on the left side of his plate, the right rose in rebellion. If he chewed with his front teeth, the back ones rocked back and forth. When a tomato or raspberry seed got under them, it felt like a boulder from the Big Horns. He went for days without wearing the offending dentures, and we feared his diet would never again include buttered popcorn or juicy apples.

Pat was always forced to remove his teeth several times during a meal to make them cooperate. Like all cowboys, he was a steak eater, and he refused to give it up, store teeth or no. He would chew it until all the flavor was gone. But when it was time to swallow it, the teeth refused to let it go. Pat would gag, turn blue, and leave the table to cuss them out back of the cookhouse. During one such session, he hurled the teeth as far into the brush as he could throw them. When he cooled down, he had to search all the next morning before he found them safely nestled under a sagebrush.

The next time Pat's teeth came up missing, all the N Bar N outfit were out looking for them. They hunted in the irrigation ditch running through the garden, around the rows of vegetables and in the chicken yard.

No teeth.

Come dinner time Pat's choppers were still missing. He struggled silently through his roast beef. Late that afternoon Etta finally found them when she dumped a bushel of string beans to snap for supper. As Pat stooped to pick beans, his teeth must have fallen from his pocket into the basket.

''You know, ma'am, it just ain't right for a man to have to hold them gawdam things in his mouth, let alone try to eat with them,'' he often complained. I restrained myself from reminding him that his dental work might have been more successful if he had had it done sooner.

When he wasn't battling his teeth, Pat spent the summer growing abundant crops of vegetables and berries. Etta refused to have any part of the canning, preserving, and pickling; consequently, those jobs were all dumped in my unwilling lap. Whenever Pat came up the walk with a sack over his shoulder or a basket under his arm, I knew it was filled with something to be preserved, canned, pickled, or dried, and I wanted to hide behind a boulder in the Big Horn Mountains.

''You know, ma'am,'' Pat told me one morning, ''my peas are jus' a bustin' to be canned. You gotta do something about it.'' I couldn't turn a deaf ear; he had worked so many back-breaking hours in his garden. But I was already doing more canning than any woman in her right mind. I suggested that Etta might help if he offered to do something for her in return.

''I already asked her, ma'am, and she chased me out of

the cookhouse with a broom. She said she didn't come here to can peas.''

The pea crop had to be saved. I talked it over with John. He knew where he could get a big pressure cooker, and he would have some of the cowhands take time off to pick peas. With our outfit, such work was even less popular than milking. They would not agree to help until I had promised them a party with ice cream and cake and John had given them a day off.

The cowhands eventually saved the pea crop, but they never did learn to get along with Etta. She developed into a chronic complainer, correcting their speech, their manners, and their posture. They could not do a thing to please her.

Meals were supposed to be a time of rest and relaxation for our cowhands, a time for laughter and friendly jests. Conditions couldn't continue as they were. Another cook would have to be given her walking papers. I thought up a good excuse for letting Etta go: school would be starting before too long, and she would need time to prepare.

As it turned out, I didn't have to fire Etta. At five o'clock one morning she banged on my kitchen door. I couldn't imagine what she wanted so early. ''I'm leaving,'' she said. ''I'm all packed up and ready to go and will be picked up in a few minutes. I'd rather teach dumb kids than cook for dumb cowboys.'' She turned to leave. Before she went, though, she stopped to tell me to go to the cookhouse and prepare breakfast.

12

Lonelyhearts, Waterwagons, and Robbery at the N Bar N

One evening after Etta left, I sensed the time had come for Pete to confide in me about the woman of the Lonely Hearts. He and I were washing dishes in the cookhouse when the moment arrived.

Pete put the coffee pot back on the stove to reheat its contents. He pushed two chairs up to the kitchen table and motioned for me to sit down. Then he poured us each a cup of coffee. "You know, ma'am, I must be gettin' old. I used to be able to ride clear around the lake pasture without gettin' tired. Now I can only ride half way round and back. I've decided it's about time I got married, while I'm still a-kickin'."

"Do you have anyone in particular in mind?" Here it comes, I thought.

"Yes, ma'am, I do. I've got to tell you somethin' that's been a-botherin' me for a long time." He took a sip of hot coffee, wiped his mouth with the back of his hand, scratched his bald head, and burst out, "It's a-gonna happen soon and I need yore help!"

"Of course, Pete. I'll do anything I can to help you."

"Wal, there is one thing you kin do. I've been writin' to a gal named Minnie Hanson in Chicago. I found her name in a magazine the boys give me called *Lonely Hearts*. If ever there was a lonely heart, it's me. It's time I settled down. I jus' can't keep ridin' the range forever."

The most startling news was that Minnie was coming to town the next Saturday and Pete was to meet her at the bus station. "Pete! What will you do with her? You know you can't bring her to the ranch!"

"I've rented her a room in town for the time bein'. Then I guess we'll git married and live there until I kin do somethin' else. But I'd like to keep workin' here at the ranch until I can find a job in town. He looked at me searchingly. "Ma'am, that old Ford of mine will never make it into town to meet the bus. Will you drive me?"

I couldn't turn him down, but I did think to tell him not to mention his bride's arrival to anyone else at the N Bar N. It was lucky I did.

Saturday morning early, Pete knocked at my door. He was dressed in his best bib and tucker, and his boots were shined bright as a new bucket. His black fringe of hair had been brushed smooth and shiny, and his bald head was covered by a hat I had never seen before.

He was a nervous wreck. "What're you going to do about the boys and the eatin' and all?" I assured him Pat could help me until I found a new cook. We drove out by the back road.

The bus from the East was to arrive at nine o'clock. We had a half hour wait. Pete paced back and forth in front of the bus station, looking and listening for any sign of the bus.

When it arrived, I stayed in the background. Pete waited at the curb by the door, watching the passengers step down. There were two, both men. After a long minute, Pete asked the driver, "Don't you have a woman aboard who's supposed to get off here?"

The driver pointed to the rear of the bus. "She's right back there."

Pete bow-legged along outside the bus until he got to the end. Sitting unmistakably in the window above him was Minnie Hanson. Pete took off his hat, bowed stiffly, and motioned her to come out. She quickly scanned him from his feet to his big bald head. Then she stuck her nose in the air and sat there like she had a poker up her back.

Pete continued motioning for her to come out as the driver got back in his seat and closed the door, gassed the bus, and headed for the next town. The bus turned the corner and was soon out of sight.

I walked over to Pete and took his hand. Poor old cowboy! It would be a long time before he forgot about Minnie Hanson. On the way back to the N Bar N, our conversation included only three words. They were all spoken by Pete, and they were all profane.

Sunday morning John and I were sitting on the front porch sipping coffee and watching two bald eagles fly lazy circles over the chicken yard. When I saw Jack hurrying to the house, I called out to him to join us. From the look on his face, though, I could see something was very wrong. Beneath his summer tan he was deathly white.

"My God, come quick! Bud and I just brought in Old Pete hurt bad!" They had found him lying by the loading chutes in the old corral on the south range.

The boys had laid him on a pile of hay. He was obviously in pain. "Don't you worry, ma'am," he winced. "It's jus' my leg." In an instant I had forgiven him for all the trouble he had ever caused.

I ran to the house to call the doctor. With each step I said a prayer that Pete would be all right. I thought of the one time he had ever given me a gift, a red silk handkerchief with a cowgirl embroidered on one corner. With all

SUGAR
DRIED
DRIED PEACHES
DRIED

he spent on whiskey, it must have been a struggle to save money to buy me that birthday present. At the time, I had thought it was a peace offering for his antics with the gun in the bunkhouse, and I hadn't even appreciated it.

Jack and Bud carried Pete to his bunk and took off his boots. John thought Pete's leg was broken and was afraid he might also have internal injuries.

I paced the floor of the bunkhouse and waited for the doctor to arrive. Why was he taking so long? When his car finally turned into the drive, I ran out to meet him and rushed with him back to the bunkhouse.

After a long, careful examination, the doctor gave us the verdict. Pete's leg was very badly sprained but not broken. As far as could be determined, there were no internal injuries; however, Pete would have to be bedfast at least ten days until his leg was completely healed.

The doctor asked us how Pete had been injured. Only then did we realize that we didn't know what had happened to the old cowhand. When John asked Jack and Bud about the accident, they both clammed up.

During the days our crusty cowboy was recovering, he would at least be forced to stay away from the saloons in town. It would be our chance to keep Pete on the water-wagon. John talked it over with the rest of the hands, and they all agreed they would do everything they could to keep booze out of Pete's reach.

Late that afternoon John and I walked up to the bunkhouse to check on Pete. I had made up a tray of food, but it remained untouched on a table beside his bunk. Pat had been sitting with him and whispered to us that he thought Pete had "lost his think."

Before John and I went to bed that night, we walked down to the bunkhouse again to see if Pete's condition had improved. Instead, he was worse. He was delirious, and it took both Jack and Bud to hold him on his bunk. When we heard his ramblings we were even more concerned than ever. Over and over he muttered, "I'll break you, I'll break you, I'll break you if you kill me." We could not imagine who was going to break whom or how.

So long as the cowhands remained mute, our only way to find out what had happened would be to wait until Pete could tell us. We decided to bide our time.

Pete finally confessed early one evening when he had recovered enough to sit up in his chair. I had taken supper to him. After he ate, he pushed the tray aside and said, "I know, Boss, you told us to keep that black stallion away from our good mares after you went to Iowa and bought that fancy stud, Cedric Footprint. But I wanted to show them young bucks that I could still break a horse. I wanted to show them that my bronc-bustin' days ain't over.

"But that wild stallion was too much for me. He rared up and come down on my leg. Guess I ain't as young as I used to be. I know you and the missis won't want me here on the ranch no more, Boss. I guess I'll jus' get the old Ford a-runnin' and head for Missery."

I looked at John. He read my thoughts and nodded. "Pete, you are not going to Missouri. You're going to stay right here at the N Bar N. This is your home. But don't you ever go over my head and do anything like this again."

If the eyes of a broken-down old bronco buster can show emotion, Pete's did that evening. Nothing more was said. We left Pete sitting in his chair, happier—we hoped—knowing that he was forgiven and would always be a part of our outfit.

Later in the evening I heard a distant shot. It came from the old corral. As fast as I could I ran to a high knoll. Down in the corral where Pete had crashed the wild stallion I saw Jack. A rifle was raised to his shoulder. Rearing before him was the beautiful black stallion. The rifle cracked again and again, until the dynamic beast toppled to the ground. His satiny body jerked convulsively. Again and again he threw his head from side to side in the dust of the corral.

Physically ill, I ran back to the ranch house and up to my bedroom. I threw myself on the bed and sobbed until I could sob no more. To think Old Pete had risked his life to prove his bronco-bustin' days were not over. He had failed, and at what a price!

Pete never mentioned the wild stallion again. He had lived in the West too long not to know what had to be done.

Late one evening while Pete was still recuperating, I took a bowl of baked custard up to the bunkhouse. It was a Saturday night, and the rest of our outfit had gone to town. The light from the bunkhouse windows cast golden squares on the sage-covered yard.

I opened the door quietly. Snoring loudly, Pete appeared to be asleep. The window by his bed was wide open, and a cool breeze blew in on him. Fearing Pete might catch his dreaded "namonya" I tip-toed over to close the window. When I had taken only a few steps, however, I saw something so frightening the custard trembled in its cup. Through the window I had caught a fleeting glimpse of a grizzly face. Then a hand appeared and crept toward Pete's throat. It was covered with coarse black hair and groping fingers.

I put my hand over my mouth to stifle a scream, and stood glued in my tracks. Scarcely breathing, I watched the hand touch Pete. It hesitated a moment, then felt its way to his pillow. Stealthily the hand dived under the pillow and brought forth an empty whiskey bottle. As silently as it had appeared, it withdrew from the window. When it next appeared, it clutched another bottle, a full one.

Not a muscle of Old Pete's face twitched; the rhythm of his snoring went unbroken. If he sensed me standing there I would never know. Nor would I ever know if he were playing 'possum.

For some time I had thought I smelled whiskey on the

old booze hound's breath. But I had attributed it to my imagination. The cowboys at the N Bar N all swore they would never take a drop to Pete—they, too, wanted him to stop drinking.

Who could be sneaking the whiskey to Pete? I thought and thought about the grizzly face before its identity finally dawned on me. It had to be Mike, Pete's drinking buddy, who lived in a cabin near the river and made his living trapping muskrats and beavers.

I knew then that Pete would go on drinking until his bald-headed old body gave out. And I gave up trying to understand that briny old cowboy. He was half-dead one minute and full of hell the next.

Pete's leg had healed when Jack made the discovery. The young hand knocked at the kitchen door one morning to deliver the startling news. The commissary had been robbed during the night. Someone had broken one of the windows with a crowbar, crawled inside, and helped himself. The most startling information of all, though, was that of all the groceries stored in the commissary only a fifty pound sack of sugar and two large boxes of dried peaches had been stolen. Since nothing more was missing, John told Jack to repair the window and forget about it.

Not long after that, Pete started limping again. He had several explanations. His old injury from the stallion had flared up. A horse had stepped on his foot. He had tripped on the bunkhouse steps. A loose corral pole had fallen against his leg.

We were left to speculate on the real cause of Pete's new injury. We could always depend on him to pull something to provide our outfit with lively conversation—like the time John gave the crew the day off to see the circus in Sheridan.

The boys got to town just in time to see the parade. Following the steaming, melodious calliope down the streets were the elephants. Pat nudged Pete and drew his attention to the huge beasts. Pete did not seem terribly interested. "Pat, you know, I can't see too good anymore. You tell me about them elephants." As best he could, Pat described how the elephants' trunks swung from side to side and how their big flat feet hit the pavement.

After the elephants came the prancing horses, ridden by painted ladies decked out in shining sequined costumes and huge plumes of every color. Suddenly Pete was all eyes. The poor, "nearly blind" old cowboy cracked Pat in the ribs with his elbow. "Look at the yellow-haired gal ridin' that white horse! Did you ever see a better lookin' leg?"

Long after Pete reinjured his own leg, young Jack finally told me confidentially what had happened. Even though John had told him to forget about the robbery at the N Bar N, Jack had other ideas. He was determined to catch the thief.

Unknown to us, Jack borrowed a bear trap from a government trapper. Padding it heavily with gunny sacks so it wouldn't cause any serious injury, he set it under the open window.

The next few days were quiet ones at the N Bar N. Then one night Jack found the trap had been sprung. Lo and behold, the next morning Pete had developed a terrible limp.

Jack and I decided right quick what the rest of the outfit didn't know wouldn't hurt them. We decided, too, what had become of the peaches and sugar. Pete and his drinking buddy, Mike, had made brandy at the N Bar N's expense.

13

Outlaws in the Cookhouse

Thursday morning as I put a huge roast in the cookhouse oven, there came a heavy pounding on the door. Looking up, I saw a large, dark man in faded Levis and broken-down boots. By his side stood a blond woman, also wearing Levis and a red checkered shirt. Both appeared to be in their middle thirties. Behind them were two little tow-headed, barefoot boys, about ten and eight years old. They all looked hungry.

"I'm Bill Hill," the man said. "Here's my wife, Bertha, and our two kids, Jimmy and Johnny. I hear you need a cook. Bertha's the best cook you ever seen, and I want a job as cowboy. My kids wanta live on a ranch. Do we get the job?"

His abruptness caught me off guard, and I asked him if he had references.

"No. Now, do we get the job?"

I had not been able to hire a cook since Etta left. What was more, I didn't know when the opportunity would arise again. I took my chances and hired the Hills. An ancient

Ford was parked in the driveway. "Get your luggage and bring it here to the cookhouse."

I told Bertha to go on roasting the meat for supper. She need not worry about dinner, as our outfit had gone to the mountain range and wouldn't be back until evening. In the meantime, I added, there was plenty of food in the larder. She should go ahead and cook her family a meal.

When I stopped at the cookhouse later to check on them, Bertha had baked chocolate pies, a large pan of biscuits, and was frying bacon and eggs. A pot of steaming coffee stood on the kitchen table. I was glad to see the hungry family eat.

If the pies tasted as luscious as they looked, I had hired a blue chip cook. Bertha saw me eyeing them and cut me a generous piece. It was excellent, smooth and flavorful. In fact, it was the best chocolate pie I ever ate. I was determined to get her recipe.

In a few days, the Hills were absorbed in the N Bar N like crackers in a bowl of soup. Bertha's cooking was all we could want, and Bill was a good cowhand. I patted myself on the back, thinking my worries at the cookhouse were over. Two weeks later, though, the Hills turned on us.

John was saddling his horse to ride out to the lake pasture. Young Jimmy ran up to him, shook his little fist, and yelled childishly, "Mister, my mom said for me to come down here and tell you to go to hell!"

John couldn't believe his ears. "What was that you said, young man?"

"I said my mom said for me to come down here and tell you to go to hell!"

John got the message. "You come with me, you little brat, and we'll see about that."

He confronted Bertha at the cookhouse. "Did you tell this kid of yours to tell me to go to hell?"

"I sure did, mister, and if you don't like it you know

what you can do!'' Then, just in case he did not know, she told him.

John could hardly control his anger. ''Now that you've told me what I can do, I'm going to tell you what you can do. You can get your old man and your kids, pack up your belongings, and get the hell off this ranch!''

Bertha strutted up to him, thumbed her nose, and screamed in his face. ''You can't fire us! There's a law, you know. You have to give us a month's notice.''

John hurried down to the ranch house to warn me about the Hills' sudden change in behavior. I had never seen him so angry. ''I think you've hired a family of outlaws. Even the kid thumbed his nose at me. And I've never heard such foul language come out of a woman's mouth.

''I'm going to town to see Sheriff Tisdale about getting these people off the ranch. None of the boys are around this morning, so you stay inside, lock the kitchen door, and keep a lookout until I get back. I have a feeling Bill Hill is hiding around here somewhere, and there's no telling what he might be up to.'' He left hurriedly with little Tommy beside him in the pickup.

The lock on the kitchen door was weak, but I had never felt it needed to be fixed. Now I wished I had. I locked it the best I could and sat down in a chair facing the cookhouse. Knowing not what might lie ahead, I shook with a feeling of fearful premonition.

Only a few minutes after John drove out of the yard, I heard someone walking on the porch. The footsteps stopped at the kitchen door. On the other side of the window stood Bill Hill.

He tried to open the door. When he found it was locked, he screamed and swore at me to let him in. I was terrified the lock would give way at any moment. But it held. After several more cursing attempts to break it, he left, yelling and calling me vile names. He must have taken for granted

that the other doors were locked, for he did not try to open them.

What were his intentions? Robbery? Rape? I shuddered and broke into a cold sweat just thinking about it. What devilish scheme might he and Bertha have cooked up? Every few minutes I summoned the courage to look out the front window, hoping to see John, but fearing I would see the Hills.

Finally John's pickup pulled into the driveway. Still trembling, I could barely tell him what had happened. John's face turned red. He swore he would find Bill Hill and kill him. I had all I could do trying to persuade him to wait until the sheriff came. Sensing something was terribly wrong, Tommy cried uncontrollably. I took him on my lap and told him everything would be all right soon.

The news from the sheriff, however, was not encouraging. John would have all he could do to get the Hills off the ranch. Bertha had been right; there was a law about giving notice.

When I told the sheriff about Bill Hill's trying to break into my kitchen and his cursing and name-calling, that was a different situation. "I'll scare hell out of them," he said. "I'll tell them if they don't leave peacefully, I'll arrest the old man for trying to break into your house."

I couldn't resist sneaking down to the cookhouse and listening under the kitchen window when the sheriff called on the Hills. His visit took them completely by surprise. "These people have been good to you," I heard him say. "You've repaid their kindness with insults and vile language, and you've nearly given a woman hysterics by trying to break into her house. I can arrest you for that."

Bill Hill said, "I didn't mean no harm. I was just trying to scare her a little. She's been so bossy to my wife with her highfalutin ideas."

"That has nothing to do with the fact that you tried to

break into her house. Now you can either get your things together and hit the road tonight or go to jail.''

Bertha asked, ''Can't we stay here until tomorrow? We have no place to go.''

''Tonight,'' the sheriff answered firmly. ''I intend to stay here until you leave.'' He made good his word and stayed until the Hills had packed their belongings into their old Ford sedan and were gone.

The sheriff advised us to keep a vigilant watch. If the Hills returned, we were to notify him at once. We were afraid they might sneak back some night to burn us out, and we warned our hands to be alert at all times.

But we never heard from the Hills again. Did they make a beeline to the next ranch that needed a cook and pull the same shenanigans? Did they work a couple weeks, get their bellies full and some money in their pockets, and move on? I can never bake Bertha's delicious chocolate pies without wondering.

14

Luella

After the Hills, I lost confidence in my ability to judge cooks. So when a pleasant-looking young woman tapped at the kitchen door, I naturally regarded her with suspicion. "Yoo hoo," she called. "How are you?" My doubts evaporated, and I liked her at once. With her brown eyes and dark, bobbed hair, she was very pretty.

"My name's Luella," she said. "I heard in town you needed a cook. I would be so grateful to get the job. I like to cook and I'm sure I can please you."

I judged her to be in her mid-twenties. She wore a black lace dress, dangling earrings, and too much makeup. "Luella, can you cook?" I asked her.

"Oh, yes ma'am, I sure can, and what's more I like to! I've always wanted to live on a ranch. I love the great open spaces, but most my life I've lived in Chicago."

More important than her friendly smile was that, perhaps, I had at last found a cook who could satisfy our cowhands. I hired her.

I had done myself proud. Luella was pretty, *and* she

could cook. On bread baking days, the spicy aroma of her cinnamon rolls and coffee cakes permeated the air. After Luella had cooked for us a month, we thought she would become a permanent fixture at the cookhouse. I was happy not to be hunting for cooks anymore, and she seemed just as happy to be with us.

One evening at the ranch house, I heard her familiar, cheerful "Yoo hoo!" She wanted the next day off. "Ma'am, would you and the boss mind if I went to the carnival in town tomorrow? I'd really like to go."

Luella stayed with Tommy when we needed a babysitter. She never complained about extra work and late hours. And she seldom left the ranch. I could not refuse. "You go to the carnival, Luella. If you'll cook the boys' dinner, I'll go up and put it on the tables. I'm sure Pat will help me cook supper and do dishes. You just go and have a good time."

John and I were getting ready for bed when Luella returned from the carnival the next evening. "Yoo hoo," she called at the kitchen door. We asked her to come in and tell us all about her day at the carnival.

"Did you have a good time?"

"Oh, yes, ma'am, I had a great time. I traveled with a carnival for several years. I was a snake charmer. Snakes like something about the moisture in my skin. I also danced in the tent for ten cents a dance. What I liked best of all, though, was doing my oriental dance. I use every muscle in my body. Wouldn't you like to see it?"

Little Tommy was all eyes and ears, but I had a hunch it would not be entertainment for a five-year-old. "Tommy, it's time for you to go to bed," I said. He pouted, then ran to the stairs and pounded his small feet on the steps to show his anger.

John and I were not prepared for what we were about to witness. Luella did a striptease, removing everything except a G-string. A wreath of delicate red roses was tattooed neatly around her navel. We tried to ignore the tattoo and concentrate on the dance. It was graceful and rhythmic. And Luella did indeed use every muscle in her body when she performed.

We thanked Luella for the entertainment. She put on her clothes and sat down. We were in for a shocker. "I'm sorry to tell you this, but I signed up for the carnival today. I just have to get back on the road. A guitar player I used to know is traveling with the show, and he convinced me I should join his act."

We tried to talk her out of leaving. John even offered her a raise. But she was determined to go.

Luella remained only one more day. Early Saturday morning she loaded her Chevy coupe with all her earthly belongings and left to join the show. When the carnival pulled up stakes, it would pass by the ranch on its way to the next town. John, Tommy, and I saw them coming and stood on the porch to watch the heavily loaded trucks drive by. At the tail end came Luella in her coupe, her guitar player sitting at her side. She tooted her horn and waved good-bye. We watched until she was out of sight.

"Well, that's the last we'll ever see of Luella," I told John. Tommy cried and ran back into the house.

Tuesday morning I was cooking wild plum butter. I heard a tapping at the kitchen door. "Yoo hoo." There stood Luella and her guitar player. Her coupe was parked in the driveway. "Do you mind if we come in?"

"Of course not, Luella! What has happened?" I pulled up two chairs and motioned for them to sit down.

"Ma'am, I'm sure no one ever comes to the N Bar N and isn't fed. We're hungry. With all the rain only a few people attended the carnival. Now we're out of money."

"You're right," I assured her. "No one ever leaves this ranch hungry. You both sit down. I'll have something for you to eat in no time." I whipped up a pan of baking powder biscuits and put a skillet of steak on the stove. I

made a pot of fresh coffee, dished up some of the plum jam, and set out a plate of sweet cream butter. So as not to embarrass them, I left them alone while they ate.

As soon as she and her guitar player finished eating, Luella found me and asked where the cowhands were working. Jack was breaking a bronc at the corral; Pete was helping Pat irrigate; and Bud was getting ready to drive to town for supplies.

"I want to tell them all good-bye," Luella said. "I'll be right back." If I remembered correctly she had already bid all the boys good-bye last time she left. But Luella hurried out of the kitchen and down to the corral.

I tried to start a conversation with the dark-skinned guitar player, but he was non-committal. His answers consisted solely of "uh huh" and "huh uh." About anything concerning Luella and himself, he was simply close-mouthed.

Through the kitchen window I had a good view of the corrals and garden. Luella walked up to Jack. I assumed they were visiting. Jack reached into his pocket and came out with a fistful of money! The same thing happened when she had rounded up Bud and Joe.

Luella returned in a happy mood. Bud had given her one of his blankets, she said, and she would have to go to the bunkhouse to get it. Then they would be on their way. When she left, I wished her and her guitar player good luck, thinking I would never hear any more about her.

I was wrong again!

A few mornings after Luella left, Pat stopped in my kitchen for his usual cup of coffee. I had scarcely poured his coffee when he blurted out, "Ma'am, you thought you knew Luella, but you didn't."

"What are you talking about, Pat?"

"Promise you won't say a word to the boss or anyone else. But there's something you oughta know." He picked up his pipe, filled the bowl, lit it, and took a few puffs before he went on. "Ma'am, that Luella didn't come here to cook. No siree! When she found out there was thirty cowhands a-workin' at the N Bar N, she jus' decided it would be a good place for her to work, too. An' I don't jus' mean cookin'. She took our dumb cowhands for all they's worth.''

Pat took another puff on his pipe. ''I told them young bucks if they burned their fingers they'd hafta blow on the blisters. You jus' come to the bunkhouse with me, ma'am, and I'll show you a path leading right up to Luella's bedroom door. By the time that woman leaves Wyoming, she'll be tattooed somewhere with the brand of every cattle outfit in the state.''

His mission accomplished, Pat took a final puff on his pipe and hobbled out the door.

15

Nellie White, Little Mother of the N Bar N

When Luella left with the carnival fall was already peeking at us from around the corner. Pat's garden had produced abundantly, and he soon would be heading to the cookhouse with more sacks and baskets of fruit and vegetables that just had to be canned, preserved, pickled, or dried. The nights were too cold for me to run hide under a boulder in the Big Horns, so it was back to the cookhouse.

I saw little of John except during half-asleep moments at daybreak when he joined the outfit for a cattle drive. The cattle grazing in the mountains had to be brought down to the home ranch for winter feeding.

One Monday morning my spirits were as damp as the week's wash. I was just plain tired. I was tired of hiring and firing cooks. I was tired of making excuses to John and the outfit for the meals' inadequacies. I was tired of its being taken for granted that every time we needed a cook I would drop everything to rush up to the cookhouse and help Pete.

Occasionally Pat would lend a hand at the cookhouse when he could take time off from his job as henwrangler. But today I was alone in the kitchen with Pete. I had just decided to go on strike when John drove into the ranch yard. A woman sat on the seat beside him.

Nellie White was a short woman, a little on the plump side. Her dark hair was frosted with white, and she wore it in a soft bun on top of her head. Her face was fair with scarcely a wrinkle. Her smile would warm your heart. She was so happy and full of pep that she scarcely looked the sixty years old she admitted to being.

I had been fooled so many times, but this time I felt sure we had found a cook we could trust and who would fulfill our needs. Rather anxiously John and I watched to see how our cowhands would react to the older woman. Our minds were soon put to rest, for Nellie became established as easily and as solidly as if she had always been at the N Bar N. We found more to praise about apple-cheeked, gingham-aproned Nellie every day. She was a creative soul and had the disposition of a saint.

Nellie proved to be a gem of a cook, too. Her meals were a gourmet's delight. Although our cowhands had eaten what they called "fancy grub" like Chuck's, they preferred Nellie's, for all her cooking was seasoned with affection. Each day spicy, tangy aromas floated down to us from Nellie's kitchen, forecasting the delights in store for the cowhands.

Now I could sleep as late as I wanted in the morning. No longer would I have to drag my weary body to the cookhouse at four-thirty. No longer would I have to answer that same old question from Pete, "What we goin' to cook today?" No longer would the boys drop by my ranch house kitchen for a snack when they couldn't eat the cook's meals.

Soon the cookhouse windows were clean and sparkling

and gay with blooming plants. Down came the fly-specked calendars. Up went colorful pictures. Lace doilies gave warmth to the once bleak rooms.

The cowhands loved Nellie, perhaps because she reminded them of home and mother. In fact, she soon became our little matron of the ranch, our mother confessor. Each of us ran to the cookhouse with our troubles, and no matter how many of our woes she shared, Nellie's shoulders never sagged.

Nellie's pies were culinary masterpieces. On Sundays there were butterscotch pies with meringue two inches high and custard pies made from fresh eggs and rich Jersey milk. On weekdays she baked fruit pies with fresh apples, wild gooseberries, or strawberries from Pat's garden. She slashed the crusts to resemble our ranch brands or one of the cowboys' initials. Bright red and purple juices sneaked tantalizingly up through the slashes.

Nellie had little use for canned pumpkin. Her pies were made from Pat's golden, home-grown variety. Each had a deep, mouth-watering flavor. Nellie's pie crusts were inevitably tender and flaky, and all had, as the boys expressed it, "plenty of guts."

Nellie's mince pies were gastronomic wonders. She made her own mincemeat with ripe juicy apples, seeded raisins, lean beef, spices, and a generous supply of brandy. Even in its prime, the mincemeat Pat had found that day in the cave could not have compared to Nellie's.

Sometimes Nellie filled leftover crust with thick sweet cream, sugar, flour, and a sprinkling of cinnamon. Baked golden brown, they were Pat's favorite. He would eat a large piece, smack his lips, and pronounce, "Yup, Nellie, now that's pie!"

Nellie baked all the pies for our ranch parties and picnics. On such occasions she baked all varieties. John and I studied them carefully before making our choice. I would whisper to him that the deep-dish apple looked especially good. But I couldn't lure him away from the wild gooseberry. Then I would nudge him and whisper that it must be an optical illusion, but the butterscotch looked even better.

I often watched Nellie bending over the oven, removing the golden discs of pie, her sweet face flushed from the heat and her thoughts on how much the boys would enjoy them at supper. On pie days, the tempting savor filled the air. Every cowpoke within smelling distance would just "happen by" and amble into the cookhouse with the flimsiest of excuses. Nellie would set each of them at the kitchen table, cut him a huge wedge of warm pie, and pour him a cup of hot coffee.

To Pat's delight, Nellie took over all the work of preserving and canning the bounty from his garden. No matter how much he brought, she never turned him down. Her bread and butter, dill, spiced beet, and watermelon pickles were a far cry from the cooked beets splashed with vinegar that other cooks had dubbed "pickles."

A pot of coffee on the back of the cookhouse stove always awaited any weary cowboy who dropped in, morning, noon, or night. A large kettle of soup constantly simmered beside the coffee pot. Nellie laughed and said she put everything in it but the hide of a coyote. For extra flavor she threw in a bunkhouse sock.

Nellie's beautification project at the N Bar N did not stop at the cookhouse. It extended all the way to the cook's backhouse. She scrubbed the seats and floor with suds left over from her washing. A flour sack curtain was tacked over the quarter moon on the door, an empty nail keg turned upside down and covered with a doily. On the doily sat a quart jar full of long-stemmed pink paper roses. But that was not all. Around the hole she tacked soft jackrabbit skins; sitting on them was the height of luxury.

When any of the cowhands slighted Nellie's backhouse

for being "too fancy and sissy" she gently reminded them it was her relief station and they had better stay out.

Nellie cultivated the art of expressing herself in verse. Whenever we saw her with pencil and paper, we knew a poem was being born. Not a one of us was not thankful that she had become a permanent fixture at the N Bar N. Pete and I, I'm sure, appreciated her the most.

Now that Nellie was there to worry about the boys' appetites, I had more time to worry about their health. With winter coming on, I was concerned and discussed it with John. The most profound statement I could make was, "We've been lucky so far about health. I mean, with all this cold weather it's a miracle the boys haven't been sick."

John burst out laughing. "Miracle? Don't you realize you have the whole outfit too scared to get sick? The minute one of them gets the sniffles you apply your potent mustard plasters and fried onions."

It was true. At the first sign of a cold, I ordered the sneezing cowboy to bed and ran to the bunkhouse with my bag of remedies. If the mustard plasters and fried onions did not cure him, the goose grease and castor oil surely would. The boys usually got well in a hurry.

Pat was always my pillar of strength. He became especially adept at manipulating the one-handed receptacle he dubbed a "thunder mug."

Pete remained as cantankerous as ever. One bitter cold day he dropped into my kitchen to ask if I would buy something for him when I went to town. It was not an unusual request. I was accustomed to buying everything from a sack of Bull Durham to a "boiled shirt." I got out my shopping list and asked Pete what he needed.

"A coupla suits a warm underpants and shirts. The ones I got last year were too damn thin. A man would freeze his butt off tryin' to get by with 'em another winter." He shivered just thinking about it. "I jus' know I'm a-gonna git namonya if I don't git some heavier underwear. You know my Uncle Gus . . ."

"Yes, I know," I interrupted. I just couldn't bear to hear again the grim details of Uncle Gus's demise. "Pete, the first day I drive to town, I'll buy you the warm underwear."

"Well, just be sure to buy my size." I assured him I would, but he seemed to have his doubts.

John laughed when I told him about having to buy Pete's winter underwear. But I told him it was far from hilarious that the old cowboy had ridden around last winter in thirty-five-degree-below-zero weather. "He might catch pneumonia. You know Pete's Uncle Gus . . ."

"Yes, I know," John stopped me. He, too, had heard of Uncle Gus.

After supper on Wednesday night, I took the two new suits of heavy underwear up to Pete. He was ironing a plaid wool shirt collar by stretching it across the back of a bunkhouse chair. His heavy breath and weavy legs made it clear he was on one of his usual jags. He informed me he was getting ready to drive to town in his Model T.

As the old Ford had been inoperative all winter, I was not overly concerned. I left the two suits of underwear on Pete's bunk and walked back down to the ranch house. I didn't know how much trouble they were about to cause.

The next morning Pat stopped at the ranch house on his way to milk. He had been awakened early that day by Pete's muffled cries for help. Before he went to bed, the old booze hound had decided to put on his new warm underwear. Pat went to his rescue and found him squirming like a worm.

"Psst! Psst!" Pete called. "Help me get these damn things on. Or off." He had tried to put the underwear on upside down. The sleeves were pulled all the way up to his knees, and the legs dangled far below his hands. With one boot on and one off, he hopped around the bunkhouse on one foot. According to Pat, the effect was startling.

When Pete tried to pull down the "legs" they insisted on riding right back up to his knees. "She got 'em too damned little," he groused through a buttonhole. "I jus' knowed she'd get 'em too damned little! I'm a-gonna have her take these damned things back and git a bigger size."

The commotion was bound to wake some of the other cowboys. In the dim light of the kerosene lamp, they could see the two twisting figures casting grotesque shadows on the bunkhouse wall. When they turned the lamp up, Pat laughed so hard he woke the rest of the outfit. He pointed for all to see. The neck of Pete's new warm underwear circled his rump, and his old bald head was sticking out through the hole in the seat.

16

Christmas at the N Bar N

Two severe blizzards hit northern Wyoming soon after Thanksgiving. Snow piled high around the ranch buildings and on the roads, but with tractors, horses, and ample manpower, we were able to go anywhere. Pete's old Model T, however, was completely covered back of the bunkhouse, where it would sleep all winter.

Christmas was knocking at our door. We looked forward to celebrating that most beautiful and sacred of holidays. I was not so sure of Old Pete. He did not commit himself to the season one way or the other. We all worried that he might use the day as an excuse to go on a bender.

Pat had put three of his largest turkey gobblers in the feeding pen to fatten them for the holiday dinner. Unaware of their fate, they strutted like fat patroons.

When it came time for Pat to catch the gobblers, one flew out of his reach and landed on the corral fence. Old Pat took right after the bird, only to have him fly to a high cottonwood branch. Pat put out a pan of grain to entice the bird. The gobbler descended, quickly devoured the grain, and flew back up to his perch. He was smarter than Pat, and he knew it.

Pat was desperate. The only way to get that wily gobbler was to shoot him. We all realized Pat was a good shot, but we didn't think he was *that* good. Pat rushed to the bunkhouse for his rifle. He hobbled back to the cottonwood tree, aimed, and fired. Off flew Mr. Turkey's head! Pat caught the thirty-five pound bird as it fell.

Nellie and I saw the slaughter from the cookhouse window. For a moment, we couldn't tell whether Pat was carrying the turkey or the turkey was carrying Pat. Our old roundup cook plucked and dressed all three huge turkeys.

Nellie offered to make the Christmas candy, but I wanted to relieve her as much as possible. If she would bake the fruit cakes, plum puddings and mince pies, I would take care of the candy.

Pat, Jack, and Bud answered my call for volunteers. Much to my surprise, so did Pete. Jack shelled nuts. Pete beat egg whites for the divinity; then he beat the holy daylights out of the divinity. He popped corn for caramel corn and shook all the old maids to the bottom. He ground the unpopped kernels in the coffee grinder. At bedtime he poured top milk over them for a snack.

Bud kept my range at white heat until the kitchen was hot enough to roast peanuts.

I sooned learned that every cowboy had his favorite candy. Jack wanted fudge; Bud wanted caramels; Pat and Pete for once agreed on taffy. I made a huge batch of fondant and gave each of them a hunk to make anything his heart desired. Jack filled his with walnuts and dates and made rolls. Bud made bonbons and, with great effort, dipped them in sweet chocolate.

As usual, Pete had to outdo the others. He insisted on coloring his candy. I gave him my box of food coloring and warned him not to use too much. He paid no heed.

By the time he finished, his candy was bilious green or blood red or both—and lopsided. So was Pete.

Knowing taffy was their favorite, I gave the job of pulling it to Pat and Pete. They had locked horns earlier in the evening, and I hoped the job would get them back on speaking terms. It did. Pete accused Pat of putting too much butter on his hands. Pat bellowed back that Pete was not using enough. I rescued the taffy just in time to save Pat's neck from being lassoed with a loop of the sticky stuff.

A few days before Christmas, John took Pete high into the Big Horns to select our tree. They could choose from thousands. The beauty they brought back was soon installed in a corner of the cookhouse's huge dining hall. There in all its majestic beauty it stood, waiting to be trimmed.

The next morning Pete knocked at my kitchen door. He took off his big hat, revealing his bald head with its coal black fringe. He switched his tobacco cud from one cheek to the other and embarked on a lengthy explanation. ''Ma'am, I never trimmed a Christmas tree. Ever since I was a little bugger, I've wanted to. I picked this here one out, you know.'' He pointed toward the cookhouse, his eyes as wistful as a child's. ''Ma'am, do you think I could trim it?''

I thought of all the lonely years he had spent cooking on roundups and driving stubborn teams to a loaded chuck wagon. I remembered his disappointment with Minnie Hanson, the Woman of the Lonely Hearts. Long ago I had forgiven him for giving me that wild horseback ride on Old Buck.

But then I remembered how he had fooled me into eating the mountain oysters. I recalled the nights he had staggered to the bunkhouse after his drunken sprees in town. I recalled the time I had sympathetically taken soup to him and ended up facing his six-shooter. It still was not easy to cover up for him when he was too sick to ride the range

or work in the cookhouse. But then Old Jim's voice returned to me: "Pete only hurts the ones he loves." And Pete was waiting so eagerly for my answer!

I gave in. "You're just the one to trim the tree. I know you'll do a beautiful job. How would you like to decorate it?"

"Real purty, ma'am, with strings of popcorn and little red cranberries and bright little angels with crowns and wings and a big silver star right on top jus' a-shinin' and a-shinin'."

Pete trimmed our tree. How I wish I could have gauged the joy in his old heart when he picked up the tiny angels in his rope calloused hands and hung them ever so gently on the tree.

Christmas morning I was awakened by snowflakes blowing against my bedroom window. Like a child I jumped out of bed and looked outside. The snow fell softly, feathery and glistening. Each of the tiny flakes had a different, beautiful pattern. If God gives His precious time to each snowflake, how much more He must give to making each of us unique. How much more of His precious love He must give us!

We were assured of a white Christmas. Snow blanketed the Big Horns, and their peaks—as always—were crowned in crystal jewels. I dressed quickly. It would be a busy day, for I had promised to help Nellie with the holiday cooking.

Again I called for volunteers. I could always depend on Pat and young Jack. Pat crushed crackers for the scalloped oysters. Jack peeled potatoes and diced apples for the salad. Together the three of us accomplished all the last minute jobs.

Nellie covered the long tables with bright red oilcloth and made centerpieces of white candles, pine cones, and frosty blue juniper berries. At six-thirty, the candles on the tree and the tables were lit, and the cookhouse was ready for Christmas dinner.

Nellie and I began putting the food on the tables. Golden brown turkeys were carved and set beside enormous platters of roast beef. Clouds of mashed potatoes floated next to bowls of rich brown gravy, sage dressing, and scalloped oysters. Candied yams, cranberry jelly, and Nellie's sweet green pickles vied with one another to add color to the table. The warming closet over the stove overflowed with sourdough biscuits and dripping sweet cream butter. On a table nearby were pies, puddings, and fruit cakes.

Our cowhands ambled in from the bunkhouse, hair slicked and faces shiny clean. Some sat on benches, others waited on their haunches. Before we sat down to our feast, Jack called me aside. He whispered that Pete had a bottle of whiskey in his hip pocket and two more under his bedroll at the bunkhouse. He planned to give the boys a few swigs after supper and raise a little hell.

Furious, I cornered the old booze hound just as he was leaving the bunkhouse. "Pete," I cried. "Surely you wouldn't want to spoil the joy and beauty of Christmas by passing around a bottle—not after you helped make candy and trimmed the tree with the little angels with wings and crowns!"

"It's jus' a little Christmas cheer, ma'am, to liven up the party a bit."

"Pete, do you really think this is the right way to celebrate the birth of our Savior?"

He thought for a moment, shook his bald head under his Stetson, and kicked at the newfallen snow. "No, ma'am, I guess I don't." In a single motion he removed the bottle from his hip pocket and threw it into the darkness. Our silence broken only by the ringing of Nellie's dinner bell, Pete followed me penitently to the cookhouse.

The cookhouse was alive that night with laughter and jokes. Our cowhands heaped their plates high.

Old Pat perched on a stool near the kitchen to be handy if Nellie needed him. Between bites he called out, "I'm sure likin' your dinner, Nellie! I'm gettin' awful' full, but I'm a-gonna have another piece of that mince pie.''

Dear Old Jim had walked across the range through three feet of snow to join us. Some of our jolly cowhands asked him where he had been keeping himself. ''Well, I'll tell you,'' Jim answered with that familiar twinkle in his eye. He held a forkful of plum pudding suspended in the air. ''During that heavy snow we had, I couldn't git out and was cabin-bound for two weeks. I run outa grub and all I had to eat was jackrabbits. I et so many a them damned rabbits that ever time I stepped outside, my dogs started chasin' me.''

So it was, joke after joke while the candles cast our dancing silhouettes on the dining room walls.

It had been a good year for all of us at the N Bar N. Cattle prices were up. We had only a few accidents other than Pete's sprained leg. We were all strong and healthy. Now our outfit was all together for an evening of entertainment. One of the cowboys could play the fiddle, another had a mouth harp. There would be singing and visiting and exchanging gifts.

John and I left our gifts at the ranch house. We wanted a special time for our family, especially since we had bought six-year-old Tommy his first saddle. After Nellie and the boys had unwrapped their presents and thanked us for the ones we gave them, we plodded with Tommy through the heavy snow back to the ranch house.

We were not alone. Traipsing along behind were Jack and Bud and Pat. Bringing up the rear beside Tommy was that cantankerous, whiskey-guzzling, bowlegged old cowboy, Pete. It had stopped snowing and the Christmas stars twinkled down on us from heaven. My heart filled with joy.

At the ranch house, John threw fresh pine logs on the glowing embers in the fireplace. Our living room was soon aglow. After the excitement of watching Tommy receive his saddle and sending him to bed, I began the ritual of opening my gifts. There were many presents of powder and perfume. I gave John a western shirt of soft green wool. He had stretched his purse strings to give me a pink satin negligee, frothy with lace. I thanked him for it but sighed as I placed it back in the box, wondering when I would ever find time to wear it.

There was a string of crystal beads from Tommy. Jack and Bud gave me a gold chain with a tiny heart no bigger than my thumb nail. Jim remembered my swollen feet and gave me a silver belt buckle engraved with a pair of cowboy boots. From Pat I received a bread plate painted with wild strawberries and from Nellie a pair of embroidered pillow cases.

Pete's gift to me was last. It was crudely wrapped in brown paper and tied with twine. Whatever could it be? Was he playing another of his tricks? I removed the string and opened the wrapping. Inside was a note. I read it silently: "Ma'am, I want you to have somethin purty." Inside were a dozen red paper roses, chosen with obvious affection!

I thanked everyone for my gifts. While John put another log on the fire, I went to the piano and softly played "Silent Night." John joined me and we began to sing. From a far corner Jack and Bud's young voices blended with ours. Then Old Pat joined in.

From my seat at the piano I peeked over at Pete's bowed legs and glanced past his red flannel shirt to his bald dome and the heavy planes on his face. I had never before seen the soft light and gentle look there in his eyes that night. Had I at long last found a tender spot in his tough old hide? I was certain I saw a tear glistening on his weathered cheek.

When we came to the last verse of that beautiful, sacred hymn, Pete walked over to stand behind me. He bent his head low, better to see the words. Then in a voice badly off-key but beautiful to hear, he sang with us:

Jesus, Lord, at thy bir-irth,
Jee-esus, Lord, at thy birth!

THE END